# The Crisis in our Democra

CW00968561

Proposed electoral reforms for the Houses of Commons
and Lords based on Total Representation

# THE CRISIS IN OUR DEMOCRACY

Proposed electoral reforms
for the Houses of Commons and Lords
based on Total Representation

**Aharon Nathan
and Andrew Edwards**

# CONTENTS

**Chapter 3**                                    **71**
by *Andrew Edwards*

## SIMULATIONS OF TR IN THE 2010 AND 2015 ELECTIONS

**Chapter 4**                                    **105**
by *Aharon Nathan*

## HOUSE OF LORDS REFORM, INCLUDING A TR ELECTORAL SYSTEM

**EPILOGUE**                                    **121**
by *Andrew Edwards*

# INTRODUCTION
## by Andrew Edwards

## Overview

This short book summarises, develops and updates an important part of the life's work of my co-author, Aharon Nathan. I am greatly honoured that it has fallen to me to help in its preparation.

Aharon Nathan has devoted much effort and energy over many years to studying how best to promote successful, cohesive societies, with a special focus on democratic institutions and Parliamentary election systems.

In the course of these studies he has developed some specific and highly original ideas for gentle reforms to our electoral system in the UK, based on the principle of Total Representation. These would preserve the UK's precious constituency and electoral systems intact but add a limited, sensitively judged element of proportionality so as to mitigate the troublesome side-effects of pure constituency systems and provide fairer representation in Parliament for all members of the electorate while avoiding the perils of proportional representation systems.

We have worked together in recent months on refining and developing these ideas, and on how best to expound and illustrate them.

The present book distils the resulting proposals into a few pages. We hope that the proposals may be of interest to all who are concerned with the much-needed tasks of repairing our troubled Parliamentary democracy, providing appropriate representation for all members of the electorate and strengthening the all-important links between the people and those who represent them.

The book is principally concerned with the UK. It therefore focuses on how best to set about gently reforming the well-established First-Past-The-Post Constituency system and other democratic institutions which the UK has developed.

The broad principles and proposed solutions are equally relevant, however, in other democracies, including those with different starting points based on proportional representation. Aharon Nathan has indeed written separately about several of these.

## The book in summary

*Chapter One* begins by tracing the pragmatic development in the UK of the much-admired Westminster system of a representational Parliamentary democracy in which people in constituencies throughout the country elect MPs who represent them in the national Parliament and contribute on their behalf to decisions on national issues, subject to some restraints by a second Chamber, thus promoting a successful and generally cohesive society and managing differences of opinion in a way which people can accept.

It then discusses how time and circumstances have conspired in recent years to make this Westminster system, as it stands, less successful than before in promoting a cohesive society. Troublesome circumstances identified in the Chapter include low turn-outs at elections, yawning discrepancies between the balance of

MPs in Parliament and the balance of voters in the country, millions of voters whose "wasted votes" have no influence on the overall outcome, growing disenchantment among particular groups of voters, including political minorities, who feel that their views are not heard or represented in Parliament, more frequent Referendums in which MPs abdicate their responsibilities and pass them back to the people, new procedures for appointing Party leaders which are wide open to abuse, and the disturbing practice of successive Governments in packing our Parliament's second Chamber with its own supporters.

The Chapter concludes that the solution lies, not in rejecting the Westminster system in favour of some other model such as proportional representation (PR), which would destroy the vital link between voters and their Parliamentary representatives, constituency by constituency, and give small parties power and influence far beyond the support they command in the country, but rather in adding to the existing system a small yet significant element of proportionality, sensitively judged and deftly crafted.

The present system of Constituency MPs, with all its merits in terms of stability and rooted as it is in local and personal representation, would be preserved intact, but a small minority of additional "Party MP" seats would be allocated to the political Parties alongside, in proportion to their shares in "wasted" votes which do not now contribute to putting an MP in Parliament, thus tempering the unintended but troublesome side-effects of a pure constituency system listed above.

Sensitively implemented, this limited but significant addition to our present constituency system would provide representation for all members of the electorate by ensuring that every vote that is cast (with minimal exceptions) would contribute to the overall outcome of elections, in accordance with the important principle of Total Representation (TR). It would provide at the same time a greater degree of proportionality and fairness overall, enabling the House of Commons more faithfully to reflect and represent the will and expectations of the electorate as a whole and reducing the troublesome discrepancies between the balance of MPs in Parliament and the balance of voters in the country.

A gentle reform on these lines could hardly be simpler in terms of legislation or practical execution. It could (and should, we suggest) be made alongside the changes in constituency boundaries which the Boundary Commissions are mandated to complete in 2018.

Aharon Nathan has long seen a compromise solution on these lines as providing the key to a well-functioning democracy with a truly representative Parliament. The highly original practical system he proposes would draw on the strengths, and mitigate the weaknesses, of Constituency and proportional systems by fusing them ingeniously together into a simple, elegant and transparent system, intuitively sensible and fair.

If the will is there, the proposed system could readily be adopted in elections not only to the House of Commons (General Elections) but also to a reformed, elected second Chamber (the House of Lords), whose constituencies would consist (we suggest) of three House of Commons constituencies. The political Parties, too, could readily apply a similar principle of Total Representation when electing Party Leaders.

*Chapter 2* details how the proposed system could be applied in practice to General Elections to the House of Commons:

- Constituency MPs (CMPs) would be elected exactly as now on a First-Past-The-Post basis (FPTP) with the same responsibilities to represent all their constituents.

- A relatively small number of Party MP (PMP) seats would be allocated, in addition, to individual Parties in proportion to their shares in the aggregate of "wasted" votes cast in the Election which has just taken place. These "wasted" votes would consist of votes for unsuccessful candidates not elected as CMPs and probably also surplus votes or majorities which successful CMP candidates have won.

- The quotas of Party seats for each Party would then be allocated in turn to those of their candidates who have personally received the most votes in the Election until the Party's total quota of seats is taken up.

- As this implies, all CMPs or PMPs would have stood as candidates in the constituencies and been personally elected by voters. Once elected, moreover, they would all have the same Parliamentary rights and obligations.

- The total number of seats, and the ratio of CMPs to PMPs, would be for Parliament to decide. The easiest and least disruptive approach, it is suggested, would be to retain the 600 constituencies which the UK's four Boundary Commissions are already mandated to define by 2018, and 600 CMPs, but to add some PMPs alongside, perhaps 75 (giving a CMP / PMP ratio of roughly 89:11). In the interests of caution, and of minimising upheaval, relatively low numbers of PMPs would seem preferable, initially at least.

- As implied above, "wasted" votes could be defined either as votes cast for all except the winning candidate in each constituency or as these votes *plus* the majorities which the winning candidates won (ie the "surplus" votes each of them won beyond the majority of one vote over the runner-up candidate which was all they actually needed for election as the CMP). These majorities or surpluses, too, could reasonably be treated as "wasted" votes.

With provisions such as these, the UK's established and precious constituency system would be maintained, preserving the invaluable relationship at the local level between people and their MPs, but the votes of all voters would count in some degree towards electing MPs and thus be represented in the Commons. The two main national Parties would continue to be generously represented in Parliament, as would Parties representing regional or local interests. But medium-size and smaller Parties with support across the country would be more fairly and defensibly represented, thus mitigating the

6

frustrations which many people have clearly felt in recent times.

In terms of aggregates, the balance of Parties in the Commons would (as noted earlier) more closely reflect the balance of voters in the country, thus achieving a reasonable proportionality. This is especially so if "surplus" votes won by those elected as CMPs are counted as "wasted" votes as well as votes for unsuccessful CMP candidates. With pure Constituency FPTP systems, as is well known, there is always a risk that the overall balance of MPs will diverge seriously from the overall balance of votes in the country. The outcome at the aggregate national level depends crucially on how votes for particular Parties are divided between Constituencies as well as on the total numbers of people who vote for the Parties. Including "surplus" votes within the "wasted" vote totals which form the basis for allocating PMP seats to Parties would make the new system somewhat less sensitive to this division of votes between constituencies.

Chapter 2 includes another important recommendation. The political Parties too, it is suggested, should be encouraged to elect their leaders in accordance with the principle of Total Representation. Those voting in leadership elections would be *all the candidates* who had stood for the Party in the previous general election or by-election, whether or not they had been successful, *each of them casting the number of votes they had actually won in the relevant election*. So all the people who had actually voted for a particular Party in the latest election would vote for the Party Leader *by proxy* of the candidates they had voted for. The troublesome tensions and abuses associated with some of the present leadership elections, especially those where the electors are paid-up Party members, would be removed.

The Parties could implement this proposal straight away, with great advantage, if the will is there.

*Chapter 3* examines with the help of some simple simulations how a TR-adjusted system along the lines discussed would have been likely to affect the outcomes of the two most recent General Elections in the UK, in 2015 and 2010.

The Chapter stresses that the simulations necessarily come with multiple qualifications. Voter behaviour would almost certainly have been different, with higher turnout and reduced tactical voting, under a TR-adjusted system where every vote would contribute to putting an MP in Parliament. But the simulations cannot readily allow for this.

No less importantly, the outcomes under any TR-adjusted system would be sensitive to the CMP / PMP ratio, or the comparative numbers of CMPs and PMPs. The more PMPs there are relative to CMPs, the more closely the outcomes will resemble proportional representation. The more CMPs there are relative to PMPs, the more closely the outcomes will resemble the present Constituency FPTP system. There is no "perfect" ratio, suitable in all countries and circumstances. Parliament would need to decide what a reasonable balance would be.

The simulations illustrate these sensitivities by indicating what outcomes might have resulted in the last two general elections from three different ratios, all preserving the present total of 650 seats:
80:20 (130 PMPs),
90:10 (65 PMPs) and
88.5:11.5 (75 PMPs).

An 80:20 ratio, with no less than 130 PMPs (or 150 when there are 600 constituencies and CMPs), feels instinctively, it is suggested, like a bridge too far. The simulations confirm that this ratio, and the introduction of PMPs on this scale, could pose a significant threat to stable and effective government and greatly complicate the task of forming coalitions if coalitions should be needed, as well as being unlikely to be acceptable to Parliament in the first place. So the TR variants with a lower number of PMPs such as 75 should be seen, it is suggested, as a far better place to begin and perhaps even to end.

Another issue, already mentioned, is whether the "wasted" votes which form the basis for allocating PMP seats to Parties should include surplus successful votes (or majorities) received by candidates elected as CMPs as well as unsuccessful votes for candidates not so elected. The simulations include a fourth variant (again with 75 PMPs) to illustrate how this wider definition of wasted votes would have affected outcomes in the 2010 and 2015 Elections.

The main points which emerge from the simulations, based on 75 PMPs or thereabouts, are:

- Following the *2015 Election,* the Conservatives would not now have an overall, winner-takes-all majority, on the strength of their 37 per cent share of total votes cast, but would almost certainly have been able to form a continuing Coalition with the Liberal Democrats (Lib Dems) and if necessary another small Party. Labour could not in practice have led a Coalition.

- Following the *2010 Election*, the Conservatives and the Lib Dems could have formed the identical Coalition which they formed under the present system. The Lib Dems might have tried to form a precarious coalition with Labour instead, but this could only have worked with an unrealistic ratio of CMPs to PMPs such as 80:20 (see above) and in practice barely even then if PMP seats had been allocated (as they probably should be) in proportion to total wasted votes including surplus successful votes.

- With PMP seats allocated in proportion to *total wasted votes*, including surplus successful votes, the Conservatives would have won more seats in both Elections. They would still have needed to form Coalitions in order to secure overall majorities, but the task would have been easier.

- Following both Elections, the *medium-size and smaller Parties with national coverage* (UKIP, Lib Dems, Greens) would have won more significant and defensible levels of representation in Parliament, without threatening stable and effective government.

With the partial exception of the Lib Dems, these Parties would depend primarily on PMP seats for obtaining representation in Parliament. The more PMP seats there are, therefore, the more seats these Parties would win.

- The Scottish National Party (SNP) would have won slightly more seats in 2010 and several fewer seats in 2015, compared with the actual outcomes, but the other *regionally based Parties* would have won similar numbers of seats. All these Parties would continue to depend predominantly on CMPs for their representation in Parliament.

The Chapter points out that both the latest Elections had unusual features, with neither of the two main Parties obtaining an outright majority in 2010 and UKIP attracting so many votes in 2015. Some caution is needed, therefore, when extrapolating from these two cases to conclusions about Elections in general and future Elections in particular.

The simulations do, however, give considerable support to the expectation that, in general, with TR-adjusted systems based on around 75 PMPs, stable and effective government would continue to be possible.

Coalition Governments could be somewhat more common, though not necessarily more so than single-Party Governments.

By the same token, Majority Party Governments able to govern without serious Parliamentary constraints could be somewhat less common, while probably remaining a familiar feature of the scene so long as there continue to be two dominant Parties.

More certain are the implications for medium-size Parties with national coverage. For the first time ever, such Parties would obtain respectable and defensible numbers of Parliamentary seats. In addition, all voters would have some measure of representation in Parliament; and people throughout the country (not just voters in marginal constituencies) would have a real incentive to vote and feel that their votes mattered.

The final section of Chapter 3 acknowledges that the many people in the UK who see Coalition Governments as a recipe for instability and weak government may feel that any additions to the present constituency system which might even slightly increase the frequency of such Governments (as TR additions might possibly do) should be resisted.

The Chapter suggests, however, that this conventional wisdom on Coalition Governments needs to be revisited. There is much evidence to suggest that such Governments can be seriously beneficial as well, not least in promoting a broader national consensus around the centre ground and restraining the largest Party from putting its own agenda and prejudices ahead of this. A non-political Ministry of Justice Study published in 2008[1] found it hard to detect any difference, in terms of stability and effective government, between FPTP systems and more proportional systems.

---

[1] *The Governance of Britain. Review of Voting systems: The experience of new voting systems in the UK since 1997*, Cm 7304, presented to Parliament by the Lord Chancellor and Secretary of State for Justice, January 2008.

On the other side of the argument, some limited TR-based additions could mitigate some of the unintended side-effects which result from our present Constituency FPTP system on its own. The present system may award winner-takes-all status to a Party supported by less than 37 per cent of voters (as happened in 2015). It also habitually denies or minimises representation to supporters of medium-sized Parties and leaves many, perhaps most, of the electorate feeling that their votes count for nothing. Such shortcomings, it is suggested, are seriously troublesome, positively inviting social trouble and unrest.

*Chapter 4* discusses how the House of Lords could and should be transformed into a democratically elected Chamber rather than an appointed Chamber which Governments have traditionally packed with their own supporters, thus undermining the whole purpose of having such a Chamber.

A system of regional constituencies (each consisting of three Commons constituencies so as to make the reform as simple as possible in practical terms) could be used to elect 200 Regional Lords, and "wasted" votes could be used as a basis for proportional allocation of up to 100 Party Lords alongside, thus securing Total Representation. A relatively high ratio of Party Lords to Regional Lords and special arrangements to facilitate a continuing tradition of independent cross-benchers could continue to give the Lords a different and distinctive voice. The Chapter also suggests sensitive arrangements for transition.

## Commentary

As the above summary indicates, the book includes some highly original insights and practical suggestions on a range of seriously important subjects. We hope, therefore, that it may reach a wide and sympathetic audience. There are just a few reflections which I would add.

First, it is important to emphasise that the main TR proposal is *not about scrapping the UK's present, tried and tested Constituency FPTP electoral model,* the much-respected Westminster system.

Rather, it is about *preserving and improving the system, by making a limited yet significant addition at the margin* so as to avoid some unintended but troublesome side-effects which threaten to bring the whole system into disrepute and even undermine public belief in Parliamentary democracy. That is the point when power would more decisively shift from Parliament at Westminster to demonstrations in Trafalgar Square and town squares across the country.

As already explained, the gentle reform we suggest would add a small number of Party MPs, probably around 75, allocated in proportion to the wasted votes cast by the electorate, to a House of Commons which would remain predominantly a Chamber of Constituency MPs. Even a small such addition has the potential to transform something indefensible and divisive into something defensible and constructive.

Second, I hope that readers of these pages will remember that there is *no such thing as an ideal system for elections to national Parliaments which will work perfectly for all countries at all times.* With all systems, and TR-based systems not least, practical adjustments and compromises are likely to be needed when they are introduced, followed by further adjustments over time in response to changing circumstances.

The issue is rather (as in Churchill's famous dictum on democracy itself) whether there is any better system for electing national Parliaments, and in our case any system which is more in tune with our past history and traditions, than a TR-adjusted Westminster system on the lines proposed. It is not obvious that there is. One can only regret, therefore, that neither in the UK nor in other countries (with the possible exception of Israel) has a system on these lines so far been seriously considered, much less introduced.

Third, there is an issue over the *timing* of any changes to our present system.

In principle, there must be a powerful case for "action this day", to use another Churchillian phrase. It is hard to justify any delay in reforming a status quo which is so manifestly indefensible in terms of the overall results it produces. Witness the following results from the 2015 Election quoted in Chapter 1:

- UKIP, with nearly 4 million [3,881,1129] votes, have one MP
- The Greens, too, with over a million votes [1,157,613], have one MP
- The Lib-Dems, with nearly 2½ million [2,415,888] votes, have 8 MPs

- The SNP, with fewer than 1½ million [1,454,436] votes (many fewer than either UKIP or the Lib Dems), have no fewer than 56 MPs.

In terms of legislation and practical execution, the reforms commended in Chapters 2 and 3 could readily be introduced, if Parliament so decides, alongside the change to 600 constituencies on which the Boundary Commissions are already working with a view to decisions in 2018.

With regard to legislation, Parliament could make provision for such reforms in a normal Act of Parliament. In practical terms, voters would vote for MPs, constituency by constituency, in exactly the same way as now, and there would be no need to change the new constituencies now being mapped by the Boundary Commissions.

We have of course at the same time to recognise that obtaining agreement even to a gentle reform such as this, sensitively developed as it may be and extraordinarily simple to introduce in terms of legislation and practical execution, alongside the new constituency boundaries, is bound to be a challenge.

Parliament, Government and Parties would all wish, quite understandably, to receive, examine and discuss in depth any proposals for reform in this area before agreeing to them.

Individual Parties when presented with such proposals would naturally want to examine them closely before supporting them. Party members would instinctively reach for their calculators so as to assess how their Party's fortunes would be affected in the shorter term. Parties which believe they would win fewer seats would then instinctively devote their energies to objecting and blocking the reforms.

Others, too, who are concerned for the country's welfare would undoubtedly want enough time to examine such proposals carefully and listen to, or take part in, public discussion on them.

We have no doubt, however, that Parliament could, and ultimately will, rise to the challenge. There are, we believe, many MPs, and countless others besides, for whom the issues of a well-functioning democracy and social cohesion run even deeper, and are even more important, than short-term Party and political interests. There is only so far, we venture to think, that MPs will ultimately go in defending a status quo which, for all its merits, is so manifestly indefensible in terms of the overall results it produces.

## The case for an Independent Commission

The issue remains, however: how can these fundamental issues be brought promptly on to the political agenda and receive the attention they deserve in time to be implemented at the next General Election?

We believe the answer must lie in the prompt establishment by Parliament of a high-powered Independent Commission with a remit to review the issues of representation and other problems which presently beset our democratic institutions, practices and electoral systems, and to identify sensible options for reform - evolutionary and non-disruptive options such as those discussed in this book not least - with due assessment of their merits and demerits. The Commission's terms of reference should preferably include all the connected issues discussed in this book.

Such a Commission should be set up, we suggest, as soon as possible with a firm mandate to report back within one year so as to enable a sensitively reformed system to be implemented alongside the re-drawn constituencies and ahead of the probable date of the next General Election.

In practical terms, and especially in present circumstances, it would be much easier to reach agreement on setting up such a Commission than on an immediate change to a revised electoral system. Establishment of a Commission could help people across the political spectrum to focus on the critical issues of a well-functioning democracy and social cohesion as against short term political expediency. It could bring salutary public pressure to bear on all concerned to think seriously about matters which are even more fundamental than Party politics.

Some might object that there has already in living memory been a Commission which considered the issue of electoral reform and there was even a Referendum on the subject in 2011.

The fact is, however, that 20 years have passed since any British Government last commissioned a serious assessment of the options for strengthening the country's electoral system. The last such assessment was the Jenkins

Commission Report of December 1998[2] which the incoming Labour Government commissioned in the previous year with support from the Lib Dems.

The Ministry of Justice Command Paper of January 2008, valuable as it was, is no more than a factual summary by officials of the Jenkins Report and what had happened since its publication across the range of electoral systems in the UK, studiously avoiding any new assessment of issues needing to be addressed, much less offering any options for change or recommendations. Other Reports in recent years have mostly been concerned with House of Lords reform.

Since publication of the Jenkins Commission Report, moreover, much of concern has happened, and the Report was anyway very far from offering the last word on the subject of electoral reform. It was, indeed, a serious disappointment.

Ignoring the telling criticisms of one of its members, Lord Alexander, the Commission recommended that CMPs should be elected using the Alternative Vote system (AV), under which voters rank candidates in order of preference on the ballot paper and candidates receiving the fewest first-preference votes progressively drop out (their votes being transferred to their second preference candidates) until such time as one candidate receives more votes than the other candidates put together.

Lord Alexander pointed out that this somewhat complicated system was not only unnecessary in the

---

[2] *Report of the Independent Commission on the Voting System* chaired by Lord Jenkins, October 1998.

context of a system where elected MPs represent all their constituents but also erred (among other things) in giving special weight to the second preferences of those who voted for the least successful candidates (but not of those who voted for the other candidates).

Acknowledging that these proposals would do nothing to address the issue of obtaining a reasonable proportionality at the national level, the Jenkins Commission proposed that extra "Top-Up" MPs should be elected as well from Party lists, perhaps 15 to 20 per cent of the total MPs, their election being based on the number of second preference votes won by each Party in a hundred or so newly defined Top-Up areas of the country, divided by the number of CMPs elected for the area plus one!

As discussed earlier, there is much to be said for having some kind of corrective or top-up arrangement to ensure reasonable representation and proportionality. A TR-adjusted constituency system would provide just that. Not surprisingly, however, the extraordinarily complicated top-up provisions which the Jenkins Commission proposed won neither understanding nor support and passed almost instantly into a sadly predictable oblivion.

More surprisingly, and against the advice of Aharon Nathan, the Lib Dems made a Referendum on the flawed AV system (without the Top-Up provision) a condition of their joining the Conservative-led Coalition Government of 2010 to 2015. The Referendum took place in May 2011 when voters decisively rejected the proposal by a majority of more than two-thirds.

The upshot is that there have been two opportunities in the past 20 years to address these issues seriously at a national level. On both occasions, however, the catches were spectacularly fumbled, and the case for establishing a new Commission to do the job properly, with due regard for recent developments, many of them disturbing, must surely be powerful.

## Referendums

The final reflections I would offer have to do with Referendums. Aharon Nathan's robust comments in Chapter 1 on the recent Scottish and EU Referendums seem to me entirely justified.

As he points out, much harm has already been done, both in the Referendums themselves and in the decisions which preceded them, by Prime Ministers who have put Party interests before wider and deeper national interests. He implies, rightly I believe, that the way these devices have been used is seriously at odds with the fine tradition of Parliamentary democracy which the UK has pioneered over the past two or three centuries, and that MPs should not lightly delegate their democratic responsibilities by referring individual matters back for decision to the people who have elected them to decide on such matters.

Any need there may be for such devices would anyway be much reduced if our electoral system was a TR-adjusted rather than a pure Constituency FPTP system.

Our particular suggestion would be that *Referendums – their use and conduct – should be another matter which the proposed Independent Commission would be asked to examine.*

For the rest, we would argue that:

- The recent Referendums on Scottish independence and EU membership should never have been staged at all, and certainly not in the way they were.

- If such Referendums *are* staged even so, then, in accordance with the UK's well established tradition of representative Parliamentary democracy, Parliament should not invite voters to make *decisions* which Parliament itself was elected to make but should rather invite them to express *opinions* or to *endorse* (or otherwise) decisions which Parliament has already taken, provisionally at least.

- Inviting the people to provide any kind of mandate (or even to endorse Parliamentary decisions) on matters of such moment *by a simple majority of votes cast on a particular day*, however wafer-thin it may be, is wholly inappropriate.

- In the spirit of total representation, a small majority one way or another should not be regarded as providing a "winner-takes-all" mandate, allowing the winning side to ignore the weight of opposing views. Suppose the majority had been a single vote. Would that have provided such a mandate?

- A close vote should be seen, rather, as an indication that the electorate has *no firm mandate to offer*, no firm or settled view on the matter put to them, and that more must be done to clarify and prepare for such a decision or endorsement.

- These issues become all the more pertinent if the choice of electors eligible to vote is arbitrary and controversial (as was particularly the case in the Scottish Referendum and to a lesser extent in the EU Referendum).

- If there are overpowering national reasons for holding Referendums on such major issues, then, in accordance with a common practice in other countries, Parliament should make clear (as it is well able to do) that no vote for change in such a Referendum will be regarded as providing a firm mandate unless it has been backed by *more than half of the total electorate* (not just those who voted) *or by two-thirds of those who voted*.

- The use of Referendums, especially when based on a simple majority of votes cast, becomes all the more damaging when one of the options proposed will in practice be irreversible and when issues of the highest national importance will inevitably be poorly understood and widely misrepresented.

- Holding Referendums in these circumstances, far from promoting social cohesion, will exacerbate divisions, differences and resentment in our society.

This book is not primarily about Referendums. The recent spate of Referendums does, however, provide yet another indication of the problems in our democracy which the book addresses and seeks to help in resolving.

# Chapter 1
## *by Aharon Nathan*

## THE EU REFERENDUM
## AND THE CRISIS IN OUR DEMOCRACY

### Introduction

To many the EU Referendum result was unexpected and to some even incomprehensible. In order to understand it we need to focus on two aspects. One has to do with the specific circumstances that immediately preceded it. The other, which is our particular concern in this Chapter, requires us to delve deeper into the wider context and the background of the political changes that brought the alien concept of Referendums into our Representative Accountable Parliamentary Democracy. Like Harold Wilson before him, David Cameron used the beguiling device of a Referendum as a means to unite and fortify his Party, seemingly without any great concern about the damage it would cause to our very own system of Parliamentary Democracy. He might have succeeded in uniting the Conservatives, temporarily at least. In the process, however, both Government and Opposition have managed to divide the country.

The reality is that the phenomenon of Referendums is a symptom of the crisis in our democracy. Whether we are in or out of the EU is an issue of political and economic policy that needs to be addressed to reflect changing circumstances. The introduction of Referendums has more enduring constitutional consequences on how we govern ourselves.

## Evolution of our Parliamentary democracy

For thousands of years communities of humans have sought social cohesion to enable them to live in peace together. Social cohesion is built on shared language, culture and moral values. This was at the root, and the underlying conclusion, of Aristotle's research into some 150 *Poleis* (City-States) which recommended that the population of a City State, *Polis*, should ideally be around 100,000 inhabitants so as to enable it to secure such lasting cohesion and govern itself consensually and peacefully. His pupil Alexander the Great shattered the idea and the cohesion it sought by creating an empire too vast and diverse to cohere in this way. In the West today, only Iceland and the Swiss Canton can be compared to Aristotle's Mediterranean *Polis*. All other countries have lost or are losing their internal cohesion, some fast, like the UK, others more slowly, like the Scandinavian countries.

Direct Democracy, as the rule of the people by the people, was possible and indeed was exercised in some *Poleis*. In ancient Athens, for example, the adult male population assembled at the city centre, the *Agora*, and decided on vital issues of state. But wars and the influx of immigration both created centrifugal forces that collided with the centripetal forces that held the society together. In Athens these centrifugal forces caused the erosion of direct democracy to the extent that Plato in his *Republic* saw Athens's great enemy, the oligarchic and dictatorial Sparta, as being closer to his conception of an ideal society governed by the philosopher ruler. Dogma and ideology replaced evolutionary practicality. Ideology, by definition, is based on the past. Thankfully Plato's dream remained a dream, indeed a nightmare, from the past.

Some 2000 years later, the pragmatic English (after 1707, the British) in response to historical circumstances re-created the concept of democracy and anchored it into the institution of a Representative Parliament. Avoiding dogmas and ideologies the British genius let this new concept and institution evolve and adapt to new circumstances that arose from time to time. The people and their rulers acted in tune if not always in harmony.

This practical approach permeated all aspects of our lives and has been reflected even in our Judiciary. Our Judges over the years tempered the dictates of the cold, rigid Law and balanced it in their verdicts with the underlying concept of equity and fairness rooted in our culture. In that process judges in one way legislated from the Bench by creating Precedents that can guide but not dictate future verdicts. This legal procedure is often followed even today. In England the Montesquieu principle of the separation of the powers of the three Arms of the State (Legislature, Executive and Judiciary) emphasised in practice the coordination as much as the separation of these powers.

By the beginning of the 20th century our country had developed a Parliamentary Representative Accountable Constituency System that guided us and allowed our democracy to continue to flourish and evolve. The two Houses of Parliament balanced each other as the House of Commons embedded within its ranks the Executive, or the Government, and the Lords embedded the Judiciary, the

Courts. Thus the three arms of the State, the Legislature, the Executive and the Judiciary moved in the same direction, representing the British people while balancing each other through peaceful co-existence with their bases. The MPs in the Commons represented the urban citizens and the rising bourgeoisie, while the hereditary Lords represented the Shires. It was taken for granted that the Constituency MP represented not his/her Party but all his/her Constituents while the Lords exercising responsibility spoke for the populations of their rural Estates and their surrounding countryside. Therefore Members of both Houses of Parliament were Representatives for the wider interests of the whole mix of their communities and not the narrow interests of their Parties or their Classes. That produced a democratic edifice, the envy of the world.

## Crumbling of our democracy

At the beginning of the 20th Century all that balanced edifice began to crack and crumble. Our political establishments themselves mindlessly began dismantling it brick by brick. This process was spurred by the deficiency in representation rooted in our Majoritarian First-Past-The-Post (FPTP) Electoral System where the winner takes all. Such a system, for all its merits, became too rigid and failed to develop the flexibility and elasticity to change with the times. MPs elected to the Commons, instead of being representatives, were substantially converted into Party Delegates.

Instead of reforming the House of Lords, moreover, so as to make it an elected chamber, the Establishment of the Commons stripped it of its substantive authority, eventually condemning it to be appointed by the very Establishment that it was meant to guide, balance and supervise.

The rot began with the Parliament Act of 1911 (with its sequel in 1949) when the power and responsibilities of the House of Lords were curtailed. Both coincided with the rise and rise of the trade unions and the Labour Party.

What concerns us here, however, is not the merits or the reasons which brought about these changes but their effect on our constitutional arrangements. Politics became polarised and adversarial. Party whipping helped in that direction. The Press and the Media simplistically followed suit and projected each policy or argument into black and white, yes or no, or "binary" in the new parlance.

Class structures, not as in Karl Marx's lexicon but the development of social groupings with shared interests, are at the root of social evolution. Socio-economic classes are stacked on top of each other with the best-off at the top and the least fortunate at the bottom. For the purposes of research and statistics the Office of National Statistics (ONS) has graded them into categories A, B, C1, C2, D, E.

Of more immediate interest than the official grading system, however, are the subjective feelings of individuals about which class they belong to or want to identify with: the Upper, Middle or Lower Classes. As social conditions evolve, individual members of each class tend to shift their position by climbing up and joining the class above. Often economic factors and levels of wealth drive these dynamic ascents. However, ideological and moral values may to a lesser extent cause movements in the opposite direction. Any mechanism that blocks such natural social evolutionary dynamics risks bringing about revolution or convulsion. In the past this was often violent; today it is given vent mostly through the ballot box.

Such convulsion has been enacted before our eyes today but we refuse to see it. Sadly the vent that is needed is too often blocked by our exclusively First-Past-The-Post system. As a result the struggle for change has tended to move *from Parliament to street, from Westminster to Trafalgar Square.*

## Revolt against the establishment

The rise of Jeremy Corbyn and his popular support as leader of the Labour Party reflect the attempt of the rising lower middle class to take what they believe to be their natural right to participate actively in the democratic process. It is a *revolt against the establishment.* This convulsion in our political system could have been contained and channelled through gradual changes in accordance with the traditional practicality for which we are justly famous. However, the gradual, evolutionary changes we needed have been obstructed by a fossilised exclusively Majoritarian electoral system which freezes the status quo and impedes gradual changes.

Paradoxically the EU Referendum results, instead of leaving the Conservatives in disarray, resulted in Labour losing its opportunity to claim the victory. If the Labour leadership had marshalled its members and supporters to push vigorously and visibly for the Remain option, while the Tory Party was divided down the middle, the Labour Party could have claimed and would indeed have been credited with the result. Instead of its declared objective of Remain, however, and instead of leading the Remain factions of all the Parties, the Labour leadership under Corbyn were busy fighting a class war with the Tories and the more middle class elements of their own Party. The EU Referendum results are deepening the rifts within the Labour Party which the 2015 Elections had already left exposed, weak, precarious and vulnerable, as well as exacerbating the wider crisis in our democracy.

It is interesting to compare the recent Labour Party leadership contest, following Miliband's instant departure from the scene, with that of 1980 following the resignation of James Callaghan. After being Prime Minister from 1976 to 1979, Callaghan continued as leader of the Labour Party for eighteen months in order to oversee an orderly transition to his preferred successor, Denis Healey, rather than his deputy, Michael Foot. Michael Howard later pursued a similar strategy, as leader of the Conservative party, after his defeat. In the Callaghan era, however, the party became bogged down in internal arguments about its procedures and future direction. *Plus ça change,* one may say, *plus c'est la même chose!* Initially, the candidates were thought likely to be Denis Healey, Peter Shore and John Silkin, but Michael Foot was persuaded to stand by left-wingers who believed that only he could defeat Healey (not defeat the Tories!). This was the last Labour leadership election to be conducted amongst Members of Parliament only. An **Electoral College** was introduced for future contests. That procedure paved the way for Corbyn to ignore the elected

Labour MPs and appeal over their heads to the wider membership (or those claiming such membership) so as to stay in power, thus reinforcing the spill-over of politics from Westminster to Trafalgar Square with all the consequences that will ensue.

We must not take the Corbyn phenomenon lightly. In supporting him many alienated young people in the Labour camp are expressing their frustration with the Establishment. Their sentiments are with Corbyn. And the more he fails to rise to the challenge, the more frustrated they will become. When assessing his support we must remember that in recent General Elections one-third of the electorate chose not to vote. How many of this third might support Corbyn or other mavericks and make a difference? The shift of responsibility for electing the Labour Party leader from Labour MPs to a college of voters has moved the centre of gravity from Parliament to the outside paid-up membership. The British genius for compromise that kept all dissents within the tent of Parliament is being eroded and is in danger of being lost.

The elected Labour MPs in the Commons misjudged the mood of their young supporters in the country. Evidently in their judgment and indeed that of many political commentators Corbyn did not measure up to his new role. With the rift between Left and Right wings however, the Party now needs an Attlee to mediate between "Erbert and Erni !" Hilary Benn could have fulfilled that role but he hastily messed it and missed it. Unless an Attlee emerges quickly, restoring unity in a fractured Labour Party will be difficult to achieve.

However, our particular concern here is the enormous impact this is going to have on our Representative Parliamentary Democracy. We must not dilute or replace the role of our elected parliamentary representatives when choosing the leaderships of political parties in Parliament.

To avoid such an outcome I wrote to The Times no less than 37 years ago, proposing a new, transparent and democratic method to elect Party Leaders. This method is more than ever needed today. I therefore quote the published letter in full below. If the method I proposed had been used for electing the Labour Leader then, *and now,* it could have avoided the turmoil that has been and is now convulsing the Labour Party.

### Letters to the Editor, The Times, 4th November 1980

### Electing Labour's leader
*From: Mr. A. Nathan*

Sir, The election of the leader of the Labour Party is of concern not only to the party itself but to all of us who value democracy in this country. May I suggest through your columns the following method of election hoping to test its merits by the reactions of your readers:

1. The leader is to be elected by Labour candidates of the last general election, ie by present Labour MPs together with all Labour candidates who failed to be elected.

2. The present procedure is to be maintained except for substituting the secret ballot by an open ballot.

3. Each elector casts the number of votes he or she officially obtained in the last general election as his or her votes for the leader.

In this method the leader is elected by all citizens who voted for Labour candidates, and therefore for the Labour Party, in the general election casting their votes *by proxy*.

That this method is both democratic and fair is self-evident and therefore any elaboration is superfluous.

Yours faithfully,
A. NATHAN
9 Highbury Road, SW19.
October 31.

## The Scottish Referendum

The Scottish referendum of September 2014 already highlighted some major troubles in our democracy. It was Tony Blair who started the process of shaking and undermining the UK Union and paved the way for that Referendum.

Anxious to perpetuate the Labour Party's dominance in Scotland and thus strengthen its position in the UK as a whole, while keeping the nationalists in check, and exploiting a seam of hatred of land-owner lairds, identified with the Conservatives, Blair revived the nationalist institution of a Scottish Parliament, thus overturning a long-established consensus between the main political Parties. The monument of a building erected to house the new Parliament brutally confirmed how far the genie had slipped out of the bottle.

Following the untimely death of the moderate, much respected Donald Dewar, the Scottish ultra-nationalists in the SNP started their campaign to replace Labour as the dominant Party in Scotland and pave the way for independence. Demands for devolution were used to unpick the 1707 Contract of the Union. No one seemed to bother with analysing the impact of the defective Additional Member System (AMS) on the three Scottish Parliament elections that followed, whose results pointed the way to the ascendency of the SNP.

Without any regard for the bigger partner, the combined English, Welsh and Northern Irish of the Union, nor to all the Scots living south of the English border, David Cameron compounded the risks to the Union, and gambled the whole future of the Union, by agreeing to hold a Referendum and also to restrict it to the those living in Scotland. He wrongly relied on Labour in Scotland to deliver. But Ed Miliband was losing credibility and with it his grip on the Labour Party in Scotland as well as in the South.

Realising late in the day that the Referendum might lead to the break-up of the Union, Cameron and Gordon Brown showered Scottish voters with promises on further devolution which they will live to regret. Disaster was averted when the Referendum produced a 55/45 majority for remaining within the Union. But the result also highlighted the resurgent strength of the SNP who have displaced Labour as the dominant Party in Scotland and have continued to use every opportunity to inch forward towards their ultimate objective of an independent Scotland.

## EU membership referendums compared

Apparently forgetting or ignoring the lessons of the Scottish Referendum (not least the lesson that no desired outcome can be taken for granted), David Cameron seems to have believed that a Referendum on EU membership would be a walkover, solving the twin problems of the deep divisions of opinion within his own Party and the threat from UKIP.

He then made the further mistake of plunging into the new Referendum instead of waiting until 2017 as he had earlier indicated. He wanted to finish it before the German and French Elections and get on with fulfilling his Manifesto while Osborne was succeeding in cutting the deficit and getting ready for the succession. In fact if he had waited for the new Governments in France and Germany after their elections he might well have squeezed better terms.

Cameron's Referendum on EU membership contrasts strikingly with that of Harold Wilson in June 1975. Wilson's Government sought confirmation that people generally supported the Heath Government's recent decision to join the Common Market as it was then called. Supported by leading Cabinet colleagues, he defended the previous Government's decision and announced his "Yes" recommendation. The country was not divided and there was a genuine desire by all the Parties to confirm the wishes of the people. At that early stage in the evolution of the European Union, moreover, the consequences of a "No" vote would have been much less far-reaching. In the event more than two-thirds of those voting voted "Yes".

We all thought at the time that this was a "one off" exercise in direct democracy, not the making of a new habit. Even that, however, contributed to undermining the authority of Parliament. When Clement Freud MP asked his constituents how they wanted him to vote following the debate in Parliament, some of them said: "Why are you asking us?! *We voted for you to vote for us*." How wise those voices were.

All over the world, government leaders want to perpetuate their rules, secure their legacies and unite and strengthen their Parties by fair means or foul. The USA is a rare example of a country that protects its leader constitutionally from this character defect by restricting the Presidency to two four-year terms. In fairness David Cameron, learning the lessons of Thatcher and Blair, announced, maybe too early, that he would not run for a third term. But he was overtaken and overwhelmed by events of his own making.

## Reason versus Emotion

Philosophers and political thinkers have tried over the ages to understand how people are swayed between Reason and Emotion.

Reason, together with logic, is in our human nature. We are born with it. Emotion on the other hand is in our acquired culture. We are tossed about between Reason and Emotion, Nature and Nurture. Our emotional responses push aside our reasoned arguments.

When reason and emotion collide, the latter usually wins. Durkheim, Freud and especially his nephew Bernays understood and explained this to us. And that is how the Public Relations (PR) Industry and "packaging" took off and grew to the point where, insidiously and subliminally, they tend now to control our responses.

So how is this question relevant to last year's EU Referendum? The answer is that while the Leavers played on emotional fears about immigration, the Remainers concentrated their efforts on reasoning about economic benefits. So we, the voters were tossed about between Reason and Emotion and, as past philosophers warned, the latter prevailed.

## So what now?

The Referendum results laid bare the crisis in our democracy. In the present political turmoil, while the Government is dealing with the nitty gritty of Brexit, Parliament should be focusing as well on the urgent need to embrace new ideas which will help rebuild social solidarity and cohesion in the UK.

There is no need to scrap existing systems and institutions or return to the proverbial drawing board. The requirement is, rather, to preserve our systems and strengthen our institutions by making some small but significant adjustments at the margin so as to restore social cohesion and avoid breaking up the UK. We need to repair our fracturing systems and institutions in three main ways.

*The first and most urgent need is to restore to the House of Commons its ability fairly to reflect and represent the will and aspirations of the electorate as a whole.*

Our present electoral system is manifestly and egregiously failing to meet this need. Excellent as the tradition of constituency MPs is, and important as it is that it should be maintained, the numbers of MPs of individual Parties in the House of Commons strikingly fail to reflect the numbers of voters in the country who voted for the Parties.

To see this, we need only to look at the evidently absurd results of the 2015 General Election:

- UKIP, with nearly 4 million [3,881,1129] votes, have one MP
- The Lib-Dems, with nearly 2½ million [2,415,888] votes, have 8 MPs
- The SNP, with less than 1½ million [1,454,436] votes (many fewer than either UKIP or the Lib Dems), have no fewer than 56 MPs.

Most of the UKIP and Lib Dem voters (over 6 million between them) are therefore effectively disenfranchised, while SNP voters are seriously over-represented. As between the main Parties, moreover, the number of MPs they have depends importantly on the distribution of their voters between constituencies, and on constituency boundaries, as well as on the total number of votes cast.

What we need to do, clearly and soon, is to reduce these disparities, and re-enfranchise the millions of disenfranchised voters whose votes are wasted, without moving to a system of pure proportional representation which would (among other things) involve totally losing our valuable constituency system. We need by these means to bring our electorate back from Trafalgar Square to Westminster and avoid the risks of accentuating tensions between classes in our society.

The best way to achieve this, in my opinion, will be to preserve our present First-Past-The-Post (FPTP) Constituency System, well established and immensely valuable as it is, but make some small yet significant adjustments at the margin, based on the principle of Total Representation (TR). I first advocated a system on these lines more than 50 years ago and have never wavered from the belief that it holds the key to a well-functioning modern democracy.

Such a system would fuse our present constituency system with an element of proportionality stopping well short of pure Proportional Representation (PR). Constituency MPs (CMPs) would be elected exactly as now for the 600 seats which the Boundary Commissions have been mandated to define by 2018. Alongside the 600 CMP seats, however, a small number of "Party MP" seats would be allocated to individual Parties in proportion to their shares in the "wasted" votes cast in the Election.

"Wasted" votes would be defined as votes which did not contribute under the Constituency FPTP system to putting an MP in Parliament. They would consist of votes cast for unsuccessful candidates *plus* (probably) surplus votes cast for successful candidates (beyond the majority of one over the nearest rival candidate needed to elect them): in effect, the majorities obtained by successful candidates.

In this way, all votes cast (with only minor exceptions) would make some contribution towards putting an MP in Parliament and the voters who cast them would all be represented in Parliament, thus delivering the principle of Total Representation (TR).

The relative weighting of Constituency and proportional elements, or in practical terms CMPs and PMPs, would be a matter for Parliament to decide. Initially at least, however, perhaps 75 Party MPs "PMPs" could be elected alongside the planned total of 600 CMPs, implying a CMP / PMP ratio of approximately 89:11.

As discussed in Chapter 2, PMPs could be elected quite simply, through the use of the same single vote as now rather than complicated preference votes, and as a pragmatic, evolutionary development (or "tweaking") of our precious constituency system without any need for drastic measures or a revolution.

The arguments for evolution, rather than revolution, are compelling. Previous attempts to change to a pure PR System have gained neither traction nor consensus. In fact such a system would have created even more instability. Evolutionary steps, on the other hand, go with the grain of our political history and temperament. In keeping with this, the great Edmund Burke's first reaction to the French Revolution in 1789 was to condemn it. Why, he asked, could those fiery French not learn from our Glorious Revolution?!

The case for my favoured solution based on TR is set out, and the practicalities of how it might best work, are summarised, in Chapter 2 of this book. Dr Ken Ritchie too has covered much of this ground in his excellent book "Fixing our Broken Democracy – The Case for Total Representation". [3]

---

[3] *Fixing our Broken Democracy, The case for "Total Representation"* by Dr. Ken Ritchie ISBN 10:147 828695-4 or ISBN 13: 978-147-828695-0

Defining a reformed system such as this is one thing; obtaining agreement to it is of course another. This is partly a matter of will, and partly of practicality. I believe the will is beginning to crystallize.

As to practicality, my understanding is that, if the will is there, the House of Commons could legislate by simple majority to introduce a TR-adjusted system along the lines proposed.

An excellent practical opportunity for introducing a properly representative TR-adjusted system was lost in the May 2011 Referendum. If the Lib Dems had demanded a Referendum on TR rather than an Alternative Vote (AV) system as their price for joining the Coalition, and the TR-adjusted system had been properly set out and explained, the electorate might well have voted in favour of such a reform. My direct appeal to their top leaders at the time fell on deaf ears and the Party suffered as a result in the General Election that followed.

Even now, I believe there to be a window of opportunity. The Boundary Commissions are presently engaged in reducing the number of constituencies from 650 to 600 in such a way as broadly to equalise the number of voters in each and eliminate the big disparities between them. So there will be visible changes anyway alongside which the suggested addition of some PMPs could fit.

Rather than ask the Boundary Commissions to re-do all their work and consultations, so as further to reduce the number of Constituencies, the simple course would clearly be to stick with the new figure of 600 Constituencies, and therefore 600 CMPs, and to add a suitable number of PMPs alongside, perhaps 75 or thereabouts as suggested above. There would then be 600 CMPs elected by the Majoritarian FPTP system as is the case now *plus* 75 PMPs (or whatever other number was decided) elected on a PR basis in proportion to the combined number of "wasted votes" in the 600 Constituency elections which did not succeed in securing any representation in Parliament.

With only minimal exceptions, every vote that is cast would count and be represented albeit with different weighting. None would be wasted.

*A second important need is that the political Parties should adopt the simple method of electing Party Leaders described in my letter, reproduced above, which The Times published on 4 Nov 1980.*

In contrast with present leadership election systems, Party leaders elected in this way would have a dual mandate from MPs and the voters who actually voted for the Party in the latest election. The scope for abuse which has marred and discredited present procedures would be removed. The proposed method is based, of course, on the same philosophy of representation which inspires TR.

Although leadership election issues are primarily for the individual political Parties to resolve, I see this reform, too, as a vital element in restoring a well-functioning Parliamentary democracy. Chapter 2 sets out my proposal in more detail.

*The third important need is to replace the present, appointed House of Lords with a smaller, elected House.*

The House of Lords would remain a Revising Chamber, retaining many of its present functions, without infringing the ultimate authority of the House of Commons. Such a reform would be a further element in restoring to Parliament its representative power.

My specific proposal would be to move to a new House of 200 elected Regional Lords "RLs" and up to 100 Party Lords "PLs", once again using a TR-adjusted constituency based method for election. This would be achieved through an evolutionary rather than revolutionary process comprising two main stages. Chapter 4 sets out and discusses my proposals, including suggestions for sensitive transitional arrangements.

All three of the reforms here advocated – on General Elections, Party Leader elections and an elected House of Lords – are based on TR principles. Such reforms would bring properly representative MPs with suitably elected Party leaders and elected Lords inside the tent of our Parliamentary democracy to represent the interests and guard the wishes of the people. They could also help, I believe, to reduce the present political unease and disarray gently and peacefully, without strife and upheavals.

# Chapter 2
## by Aharon Nathan

## AN ELECTORAL SYSTEM COMBINING CONSTITUENCIES WITH TOTAL REPRESENTATION (TR) [4]

As discussed in Chapter 1, I have never wavered from the belief which I first developed more than 50 years ago that the key to a well-functioning democracy with a truly representative Parliament lies in combining our established and esteemed First-Past-The-Post (FPTP) Constituency System with some small yet significant adjustments at the margin, based on the principle of Total Representation (TR).

### The system

The proposed system would preserve the UK's constituency and electoral systems intact but add a limited, sensitively judged element of proportionality so as to mitigate the worst side-effects of constituency systems while avoiding the perils of proportional representation systems.

Under such a system, Constituency MPs (CMPs) would continue to be elected by the people in their constituencies and would represent the interests of all of them in Parliament. Voters would continue to vote for individual people, not just the Parties to which they belong. This important feature of our present constituency system in

---

[4] This Chapter is an extensively revised, reworked and updated version of material from *A New Electoral System for Modern Times* by Aharon Nathan and Professor Ivo Skrabalo ISBN 978-184426-696-8 ERS Publications (2009)

the UK, crucial as it is in terms of a well-functioning representative Parliamentary democracy, would be maintained.

As is well known, however, a first-past-the-post (FPTP) constituency system such as we have in the UK also has serious disadvantages. While the votes cast for the successful candidate are represented in Parliament, the rest of the votes (notably those cast for the unsuccessful candidates) are left unrepresented. In many constituencies, however, the numbers of votes cast for unsuccessful candidates are substantial. Taken together, they often exceed the number of votes cast for the successful candidate.

At a national level, moreover, as a result of the way voters are divided between constituencies, the political Party which receives the most votes may not have the most MPs. More generally, the numbers of MPs of individual political Parties in the House of Commons may fail (and have indeed signally failed in recent years) to reflect the numbers of voters in the country as a whole who voted for the Parties concerned.

The TR-adjusted constituency system which this book proposes is based on the premise that, without sacrificing the constituency principle and with only minimal exceptions, every single vote cast in an election should be reflected in some representation in Parliament by contributing to the selection of Members of Parliament, directly or indirectly.

Systems of Proportional Representation (PR) do of course allow representation for all votes cast and give them equal weight (subject to any threshold levels which may be defined before any representation is permitted). But such systems, unlike the single-member constituency system, make no provision for a direct link between members of the electorate and their individual representatives in Parliament and make it difficult for regionally-based Parties to secure any representation in Parliament. The link between local people and individual MPs is broken. Representation is effected instead at the aggregate level of the Party nationally. A further, serious issue with PR systems is that they encourage small political parties and splinter groups, resulting in weak coalition governments where such groups obtain disproportionate power and influence; and factional rather than national interests then take over.

The TR-adjusted constituency system would be designed to combine, as far as possible, the positive elements of both systems in a hybrid solution. The direct link with the voter of the Constituency FPTP system would be combined with a sensitively-judged degree of proportionality stopping a long way short of pure Proportional Representation.

In order to implement the TR element, Parliament would have two classes of MP who would be equal in every respect save for the manner by which they are elected. One class would be the Constituency MPs (CMPs) who would be elected in each constituency on a FPTP basis, exactly as they are today. They would continue to fulfil their duties and obligations towards *all* their constituents, dealing with individual problems and grievances at regular meetings in the local MPs' offices (called *surgeries* in the UK) or addressing wider national issues in local public gatherings.

The other class of MP, Party MPs (PMPs), would be elected by pooling all the "wasted" votes cast for candidates in the constituencies and allocating quotas of PMP seats to individual Parties in proportion to the number of such "wasted" votes cast for their candidates across the country.

The PMP seats within the Party quotas would then be assigned to individual candidates of the Party concerned as follows. Before the election, each Party would have announced a list of all its constituency candidates. These Party lists might be arranged with the Party Leader at the top, followed by its strongest and most prominent candidates, in order to appeal to the electorate as a Party. Immediately after the Election, however, once the constituency results are declared, all the candidates elected as CMPs would drop off the Party lists, which would now consist of all the *unsuccessful* candidates re-arranged in accordance with the number of votes each of them had attracted in the constituency where he/she was competing. The candidates who had received the most votes would then be appointed as PMPs until the Party's allocated quota of PMPs had been reached. Individual PMPs too, therefore, would be directly elected by voters.

This procedure would provide added incentives for all candidates to fight for each vote in the constituencies, as this could be crucial in their being selected as PMPs if they failed to be elected as CMPs. Voters' incentives for tactical voting would likewise be much reduced.

"Wasted" votes could be defined either as the *unsuccessful* votes cast for all except the winning candidate in each constituency or as these unsuccessful votes *plus* the majorities which the winning candidates won (ie the "*surplus successful*" votes each of them won beyond the majority of one vote over the runner-up candidate which was all they actually needed for election as the CMP).

These surplus successful votes, or majorities, too, could, and probably should, be treated as "wasted" votes. This would help to align the overall balance of MPs in Parliament rather more closely with the balance of voters in the country as a whole (without going anywhere near as far in this direction as pure PR systems like that which we see in Israel, with all their attendant problems) and would go some way to correct for troublesome distortions which arise in any constituency system from the division of voters between constituencies.

Once selected, PMPs would be expected to discharge their Parliamentary duties like any other MP but would concentrate on serving the Party in Parliament, initiating new policies and bringing coherence to its legislative programmes while waiting to compete in the next election.

The relative numbers of CMPs and PMPs would be a significant issue. The more CMPs there are, the more closely the overall outcome would resemble that of the present Constituency FPTP system. The more PMPs there are, the more closely the overall outcome would resemble that of a PR system.

There is no perfect or correct ratio of CMPs to PMPs. The ratio would be a matter for judgment and political decision. The optimum ratio would be likely to vary between countries and over time.

In the UK, we already suggested in Chapter 1 that in the interests of avoiding unnecessary disruption the number of constituencies and CMPs could remain at 600, as presently planned, and that perhaps 75 PMPs could be added alongside, implying a CMP / PMP ratio of roughly 89:11. With a ratio such as this, Parliament would consist predominantly of CMPs, thus enabling a continuing high degree of government stability.

Other ratios would of course be possible. In the interests of caution, however, there is a case for having a relatively low number of PMPs, initially at least. By way of comparison, CMP / PMP ratios of 90:10 or 80:20 would mean having 67 PMPs or 150 PMPs, respectively, alongside the 600 CMPs.

The presence of a significant number of PMPs, along the lines suggested, would also help to ensure the existence in Parliament of a built-in opposition, backed by representation. Representatives of minority interests would be able to speak with authority on the floor of Parliament. Members of the majority (and therefore the government) Party and members of the minority opposition would draw their sovereign authority from the self-same body of voters in the constituencies. Both would directly represent the country's sovereign people.

Even in an extreme scenario where one Party had won *all* the constituency seats, opposition parties would win most of the PMP seats and therefore a substantial number of MPs overall. This built-in opposition within the system lies at the heart of any democracy based on genuine representation, countering in some degree the 'tyranny of the majority' that John Stuart Mill warned against.

## Representing the opposition

It is important when talking about rights, freedoms and justice in an open society to bear in mind that all these concepts revolve around the idea of effective opposition of one kind or another. The existence of such opposition is essential. Its legitimacy has to be recognized and safeguarded as an official part of representative democracy so that it may be heeded and respected by all sectors of society.

It is here that TR-adjustment of the constituency system scores highly. One of its great merits is the balance it would maintain in the results of elections between winners and losers. This is an important innovative element. Losers as well as winners would be more effectively represented than under either PR or Constituency systems. Under constituency FPTP, the big parties dominate and suppress the voices of the smaller parties and pressure groups. Under PR, small groups can keep a stranglehold on the big parties and, therefore, the government. The inbuilt balance in a TR-adjusted constituency system should go far towards rectifying both faults. The losers would become watch-dogs in the constituencies as well as in Parliament, thus preventing Government Party MPs, especially in safe seats, developing into an oligarchic establishment.

The concept of opposition in general, and political opposition in particular, is the kernel of an 'Open Society', as discussed in the famous book by the Austrian Anglophile, Karl Popper[5]. The role of the opposition is not to put permanent blocks in the way the majority of a community wants to govern. Rather, it is the door through which changes may find their way to transform society. Its absence renders a society 'closed' and backward-looking. A political system should therefore contain such a kernel, institutionalised as an integral part of the structure. This kernel must have the freedom to grow or give way to others within its wider social context.

As the above implies, any political system for representative democracy should provide specifically for permanent representation for the opposition such as will enable it to fulfil its function. This has traditionally been, and needs to remain, a key feature of the UK's political system. The familiar concept of 'Her Majesty's Opposition' might look to outsiders like a quaint, contradictory expression of British eccentricity. In fact, it is an essential ingredient of the UK's tolerant constitutional arrangements based on representation. Under this arrangement, the Government of the country and the Opposition both represent the Sovereign people. We should, therefore, not visualise the concepts of majority and minority as two static, adversarial sections of the political structure. Rather, we should see them as parts of the same structural representation of the Sovereign people, stimulating each other in a permanent ebb and flow of movement and change.

---

[5] *The Open Society and its Enemies*, by Karl Popper (1945)

More generally, democratic institutions need to be designed to accommodate changing views and circumstances as well as differences of view. This is what Popper's 'Open Society' is all about. Social changes and the constant process of adaptation to new circumstances need to be "open-ended." Without this, social malaise may occur, and society may fragment.

In my opinion, Total Representation could help in resolving such tensions by explicitly giving voices to minorities as well as the majority, losers as well as winners.

## UK and Israeli systems

The strength of a democracy is not purely a function of its method of carrying out elections. However, close observation of two countries – Israel and the United Kingdom – over the past half-century has led me to the conclusion that such systems can make a substantial difference in persuading voters that engagement with politics is worthwhile.

In both countries, around one-third of electors are not exercising their right to vote. Flawed or outdated electoral models – even within a strong democratic framework – can lead to feelings of frustration with politics and voluntary self-disenfranchisement.

The United Kingdom is the classic example of a system which prizes stability and strong government above all else. Its Constituency FPTP model has many advantages. In its pure form, however, it may (and often does) fail to reflect adequately the balance of opinion in the country and in particular the views of political minorities, who often feel they are being treated as outsiders.

Israel lies at the other end of the spectrum. Its pure form of Proportional Representation (PR) is, in theory, the fairest and most representative system in the world. In practice, however, Israeli politics has been bedevilled by instability, with minority parties able to hijack the agenda, bring down governments and distract attention from important national issues. Many people in Israel find this exasperating, but mostly they take the view that this is what has always been and nothing can be done about it. They have switched off.

Various proposals have of course been made at various times for developing hybrid systems to tackle the key issues of reasonable representation, wasted votes and stability. One of the best known of these is the Single Transferable Vote (STV) system. Typically, however, these systems sacrifice the powerful advantages of a constituency system, as well as being complicated, both in concept and in operation, and sensitive to the particular counting procedures chosen.

For my part, I have stubbornly pursued over many years the search for a practical solution. Having discussed and refined my ideas in consultation with political scientists and practitioners, I firmly believe that a Constituency system with well-judged adjustments for Total Representation (TR) offers the best way forward. Such a system would draw on the strengths, and mitigate the weaknesses, of Constituency FPTP and proportional systems by fusing them together into a simple, intelligible hybrid system, intuitively sensible and fair, that offers the prospect of stable government alongside fair representation.

## TR in practice: an illustrative example

The illustrative example which follows indicates how a TR system (or TR-adjusted constituency system) would work in practice.

*Hypothetical country parameters*
We take, as a hypothetical example, a country with
- an electorate of 12 million
- a Parliament of 200 MPs, consisting of
- 160 Constituency MPs (CMPs) representing 160 constituencies each with an electorate of around 75,000 people, and
- 40 Party MPs (PMPs), based on an 80:20 ratio decided when TR was introduced.

*Electing the CMPs*
A general election is held. 8 million people (two-thirds of the electorate) exercise their right to vote.

160 successful candidates are elected as CMPs, receiving 4 million votes in total (an average of 25,000 each), including surplus successful votes (majorities) of 1.8 million.

*Allocation of PMP seat quotas to Parties*
Unsuccessful CMP candidates in this hypothetical election received a similar number of votes in total, 4 million.

If the 40 PMP seats are allocated in proportion to *unsuccessful votes*, therefore, a PMP seat would be allocated to each Party for each 100,000 unsuccessful votes it has won (4 million votes divided by 40 seats).

If the 40 PMP seats are allocated in proportion to the *total wasted votes* of 5.8 million (unsuccessful votes of 4 million *plus* surplus successful votes of 1.8 million), a PMP seat would be allocated to each Party for each 145,000 wasted votes it won (5.8 million votes divided by 40 seats).

Further seats would be allocated to the Parties (or Party Alliances) with the most "remainder" votes beyond the multiples of 100,000 or 145,000 mentioned above until the total quota of 40 PMP seats has been allocated.

*Election of individual PMPs*
Within each Party, the unsuccessful CMP candidates who have won the most votes in the election would be selected as PMPs until the point is reached where the Party's total quota of PMP seats has been taken up.

All these calculations would be made by simple, transparent arithmetic, readily understood by anyone, without the need for complicated formulas.

**By-elections**

If a CMP (Constituency MP) resigns or dies, a by-election would be held to replace him/her. The successful candidate, the first to pass the post, would win the vacant CMP seat by a simple majority. The rest of the votes would not count in by-elections.

If a PMP (Party MP) resigns or dies, he/she would be replaced by the (previously unsuccessful) Party candidate who had won the next most votes in the latest election.

## Electing the Party Leaders

The methods for electing Party leaders which Parties have developed over the years, not least in the UK, constitute another serious fault-line in Representative Parliamentary Democracy, further (and to some extent unintentionally) deepening the troublesome disconnect between voters and Parties via their representatives in Parliament and deepening political disenchantment.

In keeping with the spirit of Representative Parliamentary Democracy and Total Representation discussed above, I suggest that Party leaders should be elected using the smooth, transparent method outlined below. This method would remove the need for primaries and for defining which Party members have the right to vote for new Leaders, with all the associated turmoil and scope for abuse. It would reduce the influence of money in politics and eliminate a very common potential source of corruption and abuse.

Any MP would be eligible to stand in the leadership contest for his/her Party if openly sponsored by a minimum of (say) 10% of the total MPs of that Party in Parliament or in smaller Parties by (say) one-third or one-quarter of the total MPs of that Party.

The supervising, counting and checking of votes cast could be entrusted to a panel of elders of the Party or to a panel of independent arbiters such as retired judges. In the case of complaint by (say) 5% of the Party's MPs, the process of election could be appealed and scrutinised by the Electoral Commission, even though this would be an internal Party election.

Those voting in the leadership election would be all the candidates who had stood for the Party concerned in the previous general election, or by-election, whether or not they had been successful. The voters would therefore include MPs and non-MPs.

The individual MPs and unsuccessful candidates would not carry equal weight. Instead, each of them would cast the number of votes that they had actually won in the last election or by-election. If, for any reason, any of them should no longer be available to exercise this duty, the chairman of his/her local constituency party might be allowed to deputise in casting these votes.

With this method, the Party Leader would be elected by proxy, indirectly, by all the supporters who had actually voted for the Party at the last general election or by-election. The MPs and unsuccessful candidates casting the votes would be expected to represent their real, committed supporters, consulting them in advance, exactly as they do when they vote on legislation in Parliament.

This method would avoid conferring the right to vote for a Party Leader partly or exclusively on the Party's signed-up or paid-up members. In the UK, widespread concerns about the associated abuses and corruption would be removed. Signing-up or paying a Party subscription (typically very small) should not buy voting rights. It would no longer be possible for particular factions within the Party, or indeed for mischievous members of other Parties, to infiltrate the rank and file of Party membership so as to ensure election of their preferred candidate.

The proposed method would confer more legitimacy on the elected Party Leaders than existing methods. It would discourage unsuccessful leadership candidates from trying to undermine the duly elected Leader. Its adoption could in recent years have spared political Parties the embarrassment of ending up with Leaders who do not faithfully reflect the opinions of genuine Party supporters.

The method could (and should, I suggest) be used to elect Party Leaders in any constituency-based electoral system, including our present Constituency FPTP system as well as a TR-adjusted system. It would not, of course, be possible under PR systems with no constituency basis.

I have long been advocating this simple and transparent procedure for electing Party Leaders. As long ago as 4th November 1980, *The Times* published a simplified version on its letters page. The letter which I wrote is reproduced in Chapter 1 above.

## Some advantages of a TR-adjusted system

As discussed earlier, a TR-adjusted constituency system would have the great advantage of maintaining a more sensitive balance between winners and losers in elections than Constituency FPTP or PR systems can offer. It would engage the entire electorate and enable Parliament to represent all shades of opinion within a more truly representative Parliamentary democracy. In my opinion its introduction and implementation would help to restore people's flagging faith in the democratic process.

The proposed system would be simple, readily understood and easy to implement. It would avoid the complications of other hybrid systems that attempt to fuse together the constituency and proportional representation models.

The system would not require the complicated mathematical formulas that characterize PR systems based on Arithmetical Democracy. These started with Thomas Hare's proposals in the 1850s to 1870s for STV (Single Transferable Vote) but were followed by D'Hondt and dozens of others with more complicated formulas designed to express the broad principle of proportionality in a precisely specified manner. The trouble, or more precisely one trouble, with such systems is that they pass over the heads of ordinary people, turning Parliament and elections into a remote domain presided over by a *clever* ruling establishment. The TR-adjusted system would bring simplicity back to the electoral process and ensure the direct involvement of all the citizens in it.

The proposed system would encourage candidates to fight for every vote, even when they feel they may not have much chance of winning a particular seat. Unsuccessful constituency candidates would be heartened by the knowledge that they might end up as PMPs – if not in that same general election, then in a future one. Since all candidates would be competing for the positions of both CMP and PMP, high-calibre candidates of one Party would be encouraged to offer themselves, and persist in doing so, even in constituencies where overwhelming support was enjoyed by another rival party, as is the case in safe seats in the UK.

Under a TR-adjusted system, the centre of gravity of political life would spread throughout the whole country, with the constituency being the central area of competition. Constituents who feel disappointed with the performance of their candidate in a general election would typically have four or five years in which to prepare his/her replacement in the following general election. With political activities diffused around different parts of the country, central political parties would be obliged to sustain their platforms by engaging local communities through their party constituency organisations. The bond between the constituency voters and their chosen candidates would be kept alive and would probably survive even when a candidate failed to secure a CMP seat.

The introduction of a TR-adjusted system would encourage smaller Parties and factions to unite into wider political groupings. By their nature and composition, such larger Parties would become more representative coalitions of interests and ideologies. So the curse of fragile and unstable government coalitions that plagues PR systems would be moved away from Parliament and into the political Parties, where it would cause less disruption to government.

With a TR-adjusted system, smaller Parties or country-wide movements could more easily gain a voice – but not a disproportionate one. Even if smaller Parties' candidates are weak in every single constituency, their aggregate votes in the country could gain them one or more PMP seats. Parties such as the Greens could fight their corner and strengthen their appeal inside the tent of the Legislature, rather than by campaigning and demonstrating in city squares.

The proposed system would remove the need for the blocking thresholds often perceived as necessary under proportional systems to prevent the disintegration of Parliament into small Parties. It is hard to reconcile such blocking devices, depriving voters as they do of their right to representation, with a representative democracy. To be effective in preventing a multiplication of small Parties with power out of all proportion to their support within the electorate, the blocking percentage needs to be very high. In Turkey, for example, it is set at 10% of the electorate. The pressure then builds up over the years and results in widespread public disaffection that may cause the system to implode. With a smaller but still substantial blocking percentage of 5%, the largest Party in Germany was obliged for decades to depend on, and make major concessions to, the third-placed or fourth-placed Party.

A constituency system with TR-adjustments, on the other hand, would have a built-in blocking mechanism. Although the voices of smaller Parties would be heard through the proportional allocation of PMPs, the predominance of CMPs would mean that such minority voices would be less able to gain undue influence. PMPs would generally need many more votes than CMPs to gain a seat.

Bringing all shades of opinion within the tent of Parliament and allowing them unrestricted access to field candidates in the constituencies would blunt the edges of fundamentalist movements and draw politics away from the extremes towards the centre. In order to increase their chances, candidates in the constituencies would naturally direct their appeal towards the centre ground.

## Differential weighting of votes

One objection levelled against hybrid systems like that which we propose is that they give different weighting to different voter categories. In general, as already noted, many fewer votes would be needed to elect CMPs than to elect PMPs. There are, however, two particular considerations which justify this.

First, the different weighting is a compromise which would help to keep a balance between two often conflicting requirements of any system: representation and stability. Retention of the constituency system and CMPs would provide stability and representation at a personal level which the UK's present system has traditionally and successfully provided but which pure PR systems cannot offer. The addition of PMPs would ensure that all voters (with only limited exceptions) have some representation in Parliament and that the balance of Parties in Parliament does not depart too far from the balance of voters in the country, thus achieving a reasonable proportionality and addressing one of the potential problems of a pure constituency system.

As discussed earlier, moreover, the ratio between CMPs and PMPs would need to be discussed and decided according to the circumstances of each country.

Second, voters who elect a candidate in the constituencies have voted for the candidate individually and not just for the Party to which he/she is affiliated. They have voted to elect this particular candidate to represent them in Parliament. It seems reasonable, therefore, that these votes should carry rather more weight than votes which are pooled and given to Parties as a whole so as to correct in some degree for unintended consequences at an aggregate level of the division of the country into constituencies.

In an historical perspective, differential weighting of votes is not a new departure. As democracy has developed, different representational weight has been given to different classes, religious leaders, property-owners or groups commanding big followings. John Stuart Mill himself, the champion and proponent of total, universal, egalitarian franchise, toyed with the idea of giving different weighting to the educated classes. But the element of weighting in TR would reflect the need to achieve a workable, acceptable fusion between constituency and proportional systems, local and national perspectives, stability and representation. It would not, of course, be based on class, culture, ethnicity or ideology.

## An historical perspective

The TR principle is based on a concept which lies at the heart of British democracy: *representation*. In Britain, democracy was founded on the famous cry: "no taxation without representation." This catchy slogan came to prominence in the American Revolution, when it was based on the fact that the House of Commons could tax the colonies without these colonies having any MP to represent them at Westminster. However, the idea that the consent of the governed was required for taxation had a longer history in England. The principle that Parliament had to approve taxation was long-established, and the summoning of such assemblies was often connected with the need to raise revenue.

In the present context, the key point is that the slogan was: "no taxation without representation" – not "without voting" or "without referendums". The concept of representation preceded and gave rise to the franchise, the right to vote.

In Britain, democracy evolved pragmatically, over time, from representation. The British people have traditionally been pragmatic in the conduct of their public affairs. They have traditionally been guided less by political theory and more by expediency and continuous adjustment to new circumstances. That was the route by which demands for adequate representation evolved into the UK's special brand of Parliamentary Democracy, or the Westminster system.

The Westminster system as it emerged was based, and continues to be based, on the right of citizens to choose representatives in a Parliament that will formulate policies and promulgate laws which are at least broadly acceptable and broadly in line with their needs and aspirations.

Historically, therefore, the British Parliament was an assembly of representatives of various regions and interests that came together and sought shared objectives in order to reach agreements based on compromise that could be imposed peacefully on a willing people. It was not designed to provide a tool which a majority could use to impose its will on a minority. Indeed, the opposite was true. This process of attempting to reach a consensual accommodation was helped over the ages by an underlying culture of fairness in the country at large, reflected by its representatives in Parliament. The concept of fairness and equity has always been, and remains even today, an overriding principle of British public life and one of the pillars of its legal and judicial system.

In their enthusiasm for off-the-shelf, *instant* democracy, many developing nations – mesmerised in some cases by the concept of Arithmetical Democracy – have rushed into embracing electoral systems without due regard to their social circumstances or the stage of their political maturity. The troublesome consequences which may result from this can be seen around the world, and they prompted Professor Roger Scruton to offer the following insight in his book "England – an Elegy":

> *'Nothing is better known about the English than the fact that they developed over the centuries a unique political system, and then planted it around the globe. Yet the nature of this system is widely misunderstood. The reason for this, I believe, is that the commentators have misidentified the fundamental principle on which the English constitution rested. Almost all popular historians and political analysts see the English system as an experiment in parliamentary democracy. In fact, however, the key notion was not democracy but representation, and it was as a means to represent the interest of the English people that we should understand the institutions of Parliament'*

The pragmatic development of democracy in Britain differed markedly from that of ancient civilisations. It was not a copy of the direct democracy of the Greek *polis* or the Roman Republic.

It also differed from the routes pursued in the countries of continental Europe. For the most part these latter countries attempted to put into practice theories based on imaginary social contracts. The ideas of thinkers such as Grotius and Rousseau directly influenced the shaping of politics in Holland and France respectively. Their counterparts in England – Hobbes, Locke, Hume and even John Stuart Mill – did not succeed in making a similarly direct impact on the practical politics of their respective times. Locke's ideas almost shaped the American political system but, although his political thinking permeated his native country, he could not claim the direct influence which continental European thinkers wielded. In Britain, the push for change came from the bottom up; it was never dictated from the top.

The contrast between the conceptualisation of democracy in Britain and continental Europe reflects not only different outlooks on society but, quite literally, different ways of thinking. Contrast the clear-cut assertive didactic Jean-Jacques Rousseau's "Social Contract" with the tentative, reflective John Stuart Mill's "On Liberty". The former proffers the diagnosis and the cure right from the start. The latter keeps the doubts and sustains a pragmatic line throughout. One wonders whether these differing approaches are embedded even in the structures of their respective languages. Or is it that the former is influenced by Greek culture and the latter by Rome? What concerns us here, however, is the effect these two approaches have had on subsequent political thinking and practice.

In the UK, the fusion of freedom of expression and the choice of representatives are at the heart of the cultural framework of representative democracy. The phrases "much might be said on both sides", or "he is entitled to his opinion" are often heard even today in the pubs and streets of Britain. These two basic ingredients – representation and freedom of expression – are closely linked and create the fluidity that makes it possible to bring about peaceful political change in tune with constantly evolving social realities.

## Arithmetical Democracy

The misunderstandings and confusions caused by the progressive decoupling of democracy from its historical roots of representation and equity have had a damaging influence on the practice of parliamentary democracy in many countries, not least those that have adopted the UK's Westminster model.

A simplistic conception of democracy based purely on arithmetic (and often employing complicated and convoluted mathematical formulas) has become the foundation of the political systems in these countries. A 51-per-cent majority of votes cast, or of MPs elected, gives the stamp of legitimacy to many such regimes around the world. Meanwhile these systems tend to ignore, or largely ignore, the important principle of catering for continuous and uninterrupted representation of the expressed interests of everyone – including the 49-

per-cent minority – from which the UK's Westminster model evolved.

The Westminster model in the UK itself has not escaped this decoupling. The pattern of representing groups and interests shifted in the twentieth century towards voting based on the numbers of individuals in adult society as a whole. Representational Democracy came closer to being Arithmetical Democracy. This trend was helped by the rapid growth of human rights movements and a growing acceptance of egalitarianism as the natural counterpart of these movements.

Of course many of these reforms were right and indeed overdue, not least the extension of the franchise to previously disenfranchised groups within society. For the most part, there is no way that these reforms can or should be reversed. There is no dispute, either, that numbers are important.

As discussed earlier, however, systems which are totally arithmetic-dominated, awarding unfettered power to a majority Party or deciding major national issues in referendums, often by wafer-thin majorities in each case, risk causing serious social malaise and tearing societies apart. The electoral system needs to mitigate, as far as possible, the resulting social and political strains by being transparently fair and sensible and appropriating a suitable degree of power and influence to losers as well as winners. That is what representation is about.

When we discuss Parliaments and constitutional issues, therefore, we need to think constantly about representation as well as democracy. As Professor Gideon Doron, the late President of the Political Association of Israel, has written in books and articles in support of the TR principle.

> *"In Democracies, voting is not just about winning and losing. It is also about Representation."*

I would urge all who research this topic to internalise this wisdom - and to remember that representation is about nipping social conflicts in the bud and holding societies together when they might otherwise fall apart. That is what the proposals in this Chapter, combining a constituency system with Total Representation, would aim to do.

# Chapter 3
## *by Andrew Edwards*

# SIMULATIONS OF TR IN THE 2010 AND 2015 ELECTIONS

## Introduction

It is natural to ask: what would the outcomes have been if a system combining the familiar Constituency FPTP system with Total Representation (TR), as proposed in Chapter 2, had been in place in recent UK General Elections? And how different would such outcomes have been from what actually happened?

The simulations in columns 3 to 6 of the accompanying Tables 1 and 2 indicate what the outcomes *might* have been in the two most recent Elections – those of 2015 and 2010 – subject to some significant qualifications about voter behaviour and on various assumptions about specification of the TR additions.

As discussed below, both Elections had unusual features. So the simulations should not be seen as providing foolproof guidance on the effects of a TR-adjusted system in future Elections.

Columns 1 and 2 of the Tables show, for comparison, what the actual outcomes were (under the present Constituency FPTP system) and what the outcomes might have been with a system of pure Proportional Representation (PR). These comparisons are of interest, not just in their own right, but also because TR itself is conceived as a sensitively judged fusion of a predominantly Constituency FPTP system with an element of PR so as to achieve a balance of stability, regional representation and proportionality which may help to promote a more successful and cohesive society.

## Qualifications and variants

As is the way with counterfactuals, any assessment of what would have happened under TR has to be qualified in various ways. Two of these are especially important.

First, *voter behaviour* would probably have been significantly different if TR additions had been in place alongside the established Constituency system. In sharp contrast with the present, pure Constituency FPTP system, virtually every vote that was cast would have contributed, to a greater or lesser degree, to putting an MP in Parliament. Members of the electorate would therefore have been more likely to vote, especially in "safe" seats where they have previously seen little point in voting. In these circumstances, turnout would probably have been higher, and "tactical" voting less significant. These are, indeed, advantages which a TR-adjusted system could have brought. Inevitably, however, the simulations do not make any allowance for such induced changes in voter behaviour.

Second, the outcomes would have been much influenced by the decisions made on *specification of the TR additions to our present system*. As discussed in the Introduction and in earlier Chapters, there is no single specification which is demonstrably "correct" or would be suitable at all times and in all circumstances. On the contrary, there would be important options within any TR system for:

- the comparative numbers of Constituency MPs (CMPs) and Party MPs (PMPs) (or the related CMP / PMP ratio) and
- whether or not the surplus successful votes (ie majorities) won by those elected as CMPs are taken into account as well as unsuccessful votes (for candidates not securing election as CMPs) in allocating PMP seats to Parties.

We have thought it right to explore some variant TR options accordingly in the simulations, rather than present a single take-it-or-leave-it case.

With regard to the balance between CMPs and PMPs, Parliament would have the opportunity to set these numbers at levels which are thought to strike a reasonable compromise between competing priorities. The higher the priority attached to stability and strength in government, regional and local representation and personal engagement between electors and elected, the more CMPs will be needed relative to PMPs. The higher the priority attached to fair representation for medium-size and smaller Parties with support across the country, and to achievement of a reasonable proportionality overall between the balance of voters in the country and the balance of MPs in Parliament, the more PMPs will be needed relative to CMPs.

To simplify more than a little, therefore, the decision on the CMP / PMP balance can be seen as reflecting a judgment on the relative importance of stable and effective government on the one hand and fair representation on the other.

73

In practice, we believe it would be important in future elections, and would have been similarly important in the 2010 and 2015 Elections, to exercise caution and moderation when leavening the UK's precious Constituency system (CMPs) with an element of proportionality (PMPs), as the addition of a TR element would do (or have done). Our present Constituency system is simple, familiar, well tried and tested and excellent in many respects. It would be seriously misguided, in our view, to tear it up or to undertake a massive, revolutionary reform when what is needed is a small but significant adjustment at the margins.

In countries such as Israel and the Netherlands, whose present systems are close to pure PR, we would similarly think it prudent, initially at least, to introduce a form of TR closer to PR which preserves the benefits of PR systems. In both cases, evolution is likely to be a far better course than revolution.

In accordance with this principle, we have begun from the premise that it would be (or would have been) misguided to flood the UK Parliament straight away (or indeed ever) with enormous numbers of PMPs. It would seem better to plan for a relatively modest, though still significant, number of PMPs. We have therefore based the simulations on three illustrative assumptions about the comparative numbers of CMPs and PMPs. In all cases the number of CMPs is constrained so as to maintain the total number of MPs (CMPs plus PMPs) at its actual level of 650, thus facilitating comparison with outcomes under our present system and with other cases. The cases illustrated are:

(a)     520 CMPs and 130 PMPs (an 80:20 ratio)
(b)     585 CMPs and 65 PMPs (a 90:10 ratio), and
(c)     575 CMPs and 75 PMPs (an 88.5: 11.5 ratio).

We believe that cases (a) and (b) may be seen as providing upper and lower bounds on what would be (or would have been) sensible in the UK, initially at least, in terms of PMP numbers.

For what it is worth, we have a strong sense that adding as many as 130 PMPs alongside 520 CMPs, as in simulation (a), would be a bridge too far. Applying the same 80:20 ratio would mean adding 150 PMPs alongside the 600 constituencies and CMPs which the Boundary Commissions are currently mandated to deliver for Elections from 2018 onwards. The simulations themselves suggest that an 80:20 ratio could produce unsettled outcomes which would, among other things, seriously complicate the task of forming Coalition Governments, if such Governments should be needed.

Adding 65 PMPs alongside 585 CMPs, as in simulation (b), feels closer to the mark, but perhaps a fraction understated.

So we have added a further simulation, case (c), with 75 PMPs and 575 CMPs. Applying a similar ratio in the next Election would mean adding a similar number of PMPs (say 75 again) alongside the 600 constituencies and CMPs proposed from 2018 onwards.

This feels instinctively like an attractive place to begin, offering the prospect of a sensible compromise between stability and local representation, on the one hand, and representation of different shades of opinion across the country and proportionality, on the other.

Within case (c), we have illustrated two sub-options for the allocation of PMP seats to Parties (thus making four TR variants in all). These seats could be (or could have been) allocated in proportion to either:

- "unsuccessful" votes (UVs) cast nationally for each Party (ie votes for candidates who did not secure election as CMPs) or

- "unsuccessful" votes *plus* "surplus successful" votes (SSVs) cast nationally for each Party, the latter being defined as the majorities won by elected CMPs beyond the majority of one vote over the runner-up candidate which would have sufficed for winning the seat.

As discussed in the Introduction and Chapter 2, "surplus successful" votes (SSVs) may likewise be regarded as "wasted" votes which ought to receive some representation, at least, in Parliament. Including such votes in the basis for allocating PMP seats would arguably, therefore, be right in principle. It would have the advantage of giving voters in safe-seat constituencies an incentive to vote which they might otherwise have lacked.

Inclusion of SSVs could also help to correct in some degree for unfair advantages or disadvantages to individual Parties resulting from the way in which their supporters are divided between constituencies. As noted in the Introduction, this is a serious problem in pure Constituency FPTP systems. The overall outcome for individual Parties depends, not just on the total number of votes they win, but also (and very importantly) on how the votes are divided between constituencies. To see how serious this problem may be, one need only note that, if voters in every constituency voted for Parties in the same ratio, then the Party winning the most votes nationally would win every seat in the country. Significantly, voting patterns and effects on overall Election outcomes do not form part of the remit of the UK's four Boundary Commissions.

For all these reasons, therefore, we have thought it right to test in a further sub-option what effect taking these surplus successful votes into account when allocating PMP seats to Parties might be expected to have had on the outcomes.

Such, then, is the basis on which we have constructed the simulations set out in Tables 1 and 2. The underlying calculations, all beautifully simple, are set out in the supporting Annex Tables A1 to A4 at the end of the Chapter. In contrast with many electoral systems introduced in recent years in other contexts and areas, and with many suggestions made for reforming the system for electing MPs, beautiful simplicity is indeed a notable feature of TR systems of the kind proposed.

Subject to the important qualification about induced changes in behaviour mentioned earlier, Table 1, with supporting Tables A1 and A2, illustrates what the outcomes might have been if various TR options had been in place for the 2015 Election. Table 2, with supporting Tables A3 and A4, gives similar illustrations for the 2010 Election.

In all the simulated TR cases, the total number of MPs (CMPs + PMPs) is maintained at 650 so as to facilitate comparisons with actual outcomes under the existing Constituency FPTP system and simulated outcomes under a pure PR system. CMP numbers are reduced below the number of MPs there actually were so as to accommodate within the 650 total the number of PMPs illustrated in each case.

The remaining sections of this Chapter discuss the main conclusions and points of interest which emerge.

## 2015 Election

In both the recent Elections, the number of MP seats and constituencies was 650. So 326 seats were needed for a majority.

*Actual outcome (Table 1, column 1)*

In the 2015 Election, as is well known, the Conservative Party actually won 331 seats, thus obtaining a small majority of 12 seats overall and removing the need for a continuing Coalition with the Liberal Democrats or any other Party. Table 1, column 1, gives the figures.

*Outcome with a pure PR system (column 2)*

With a pure Proportional Representation system, the outcome would have been markedly different, and probably unstable. The Conservatives would have fallen a long way short of winning an overall majority and would have needed a Coalition with UKIP and one other small

Party in order to govern, unless they had been prepared to form a Coalition with Labour. The Labour Party would have needed an even more improbable partnership with UKIP, the Lib Dems, the Greens and several other Parties in order to lead a Coalition. It would have been hard to avoid repeated and extended periods of stressful haggling between the Parties, probably resulting in precarious outcomes and greatly complicating the tasks of government.

*TR variants: impact on the major Parties (columns 3-6)*

Under all the variant TR specifications illustrated, the Conservatives, with between 290 and 317 seats (depending on how TR was specified), would have fallen short of winning an overall majority on the strength of their 37 per cent share of total votes cast.

With any of the three more realistic TR variant specifications in cols 4-6 of Table 1, however, providing for 65 or 75 PMPs, *the Conservatives would almost certainly have managed without great difficulty to maintain their Coalition with the Lib Dems* (albeit with support from another small Party if the 75 PMP case had been combined with allocation of PMP seat quotas on an unsuccessful-votes-only basis).

# Table 1

## UK Election 2015
Seats actually won compared with simulations of seats won under pure PR and under TR (four variants)

| System | Actual FPTP | Pure PR | TR 80:20 UV only | TR 90:10 UV only | TR 88.5 / 11.5 UV only | UV+SSV |
|---|---|---|---|---|---|---|
| CMPs/PMPs | na | na | 520/130 | 585/65 | 575/75 | 575/75 |
| Cons | 331 | 240 | 290 | 311 | 307 | 317 |
| Lab | 232 | 198 | 223 | 226 | 226 | 227 |
| UKIP | 1 | 82 | 34 | 17 | 20 | 14 |
| LD | 8 | 51 | 25 | 17 | 18 | 15 |
| SNP | 56 | 31 | 45 | 50 | 49 | 51 |
| Green | 1 | 25 | 11 | 6 | 7 | 5 |
| DUP | 8 | 4 | 7 | 7 | 7 | 7 |
| PC | 3 | 4 | 3 | 4 | 4 | 4 |
| SF | 4 | 4 | 4 | 5 | 4 | 3 |
| UUP | 2 | 2 | 3 | 2 | 3 | 2 |
| SDLP | 3 | 2 | 3 | 3 | 3 | 3 |
| Indep | 1 | 0 | 1 | 1 | 1 | 1 |
| Others | 0 | 7 | 1 | 1 | 1 | 1 |
| Totals: | 650 | 650 | 650 | 650 | 650 | 650 |

Notes:
- Total seats (CMPs+PMPs) are constrained to 650 in all TR cases so as to facilitate comparisons
- For an overall majority, a party (or Coalition) would have needed 326 seats or more
- The Conservatives actually won an overall majority of 12 seats (col 1) but would not have won an overall majority under any of the (simulated) systems in cols 2-6.
- With pure PR (col 2) either Cons or Lab could have formed a Coalition with LDs.
- The TR variants in cols 3-5 allocate PMP seats to Parties in proportion to their shares in total *unsuccessful* votes cast (UV) only, based on CMP/PMP ratios of 80:20, 90:10 and 88.5:11.5. Seats won and Coalition options would have been sensitive to the ratios chosen.
- The col 6 TR variant allocates PMP seats to Parties in proportion to their shares in *unsuccessful plus surplus successful votes* (UV+ SSV), based on a CMP/PMP ratio of 88.5:11.5. Cons would have won more seats, facilitating Coalition formation.
- In all TR cases, medium-size Parties with national coverage (UKIP, LDs, Greens) would have won significant numbers of seats.
- The effects on regional Parties would have been much more limited.
- Detailed supporting calculations are in Tables A1 and A2.

With an 80:20 CMP / PMP ratio and 130 PMPs, on the other hand, and assuming that Coalitions with Labour, the SNP or UKIP would have been seen as unacceptable, the Conservatives could have found the task of forming a Coalition very challenging. They would have needed to recruit the Greens (and preferably one or two of the Northern Ireland Unionist Parties) as well as the Lib Dems. Any Coalition they formed would probably have been precarious. They might have felt they had no option but to form a minority Government.

In the 2015 Election, therefore, an 80:20 ratio, with as many as 130 PMPs, (or 150 PMPs with 600 constituencies) would quite possibly have produced a stalemate which would have threatened stable and effective government. This supports our instinct, discussed earlier, that *introducing TR with an 80:20 ratio would be a bridge too far and that allocating 75 seats or thereabouts for PMPs would be a far better place to begin, in present circumstances at least.*

It probably goes without saying that no Party other than the Conservatives would have been able to lead a Coalition after the 2015 Election under any of the variant TR specifications considered. *The Labour Party, with between 223 and 227 seats, would not realistically have been able to lead a Coalition.*

*TR-variants: comparative definitions of wasted votes*

In this 2015 Election, allocation of PMP seats on the basis of *total wasted votes* (surplus successful votes, SSV, as well as unsuccessful votes, UV: compare cols 5 & 6 of

Table 1) would have benefited mainly the Conservative Party by giving them 10 more seats. On this basis, a Coalition led by the Conservatives would have had a more comfortable majority.

The Lib Dems would have won 6 fewer seats than on an unsuccessful-votes-only basis, thus making it still less possible for Labour to lead a Coalition.

*TR variants: impact on the medium-size Parties with wide national coverage*

Under all the TR variants considered, the *medium-size Parties with wide national coverage* - Lib Dems, Greens and UKIP - *would all have won significantly more seats than the tiny numbers they actually won*. The simulations indicate that, under the three "realistic" TR variants (columns 4 to 6 of Table 1), they would have won between 34 and 45 seats between them (rather than the 10 seats they actually won), thus achieving a much more generous and defensible level of representation than under the pure Constituency FPTP system. With the "unrealistic" 80:20 ratio, they would have won no less than 70 seats.

These Parties' seats would have consisted largely of PMP seats, which they would have won as a result of the large numbers of unsuccessful votes they attracted across the country.

The simulations confirm, therefore, what one would expect. The medium-size Parties with wide national coverage will score better, the more PMP seats there are in total. The counterpart of this is that the major Parties will score less well.

The medium-size Parties seldom win seats by large majorities. So they would win somewhat fewer seats if PMP seat quotas are allocated in proportion to total wasted votes, including surplus successful votes, not just unsuccessful votes.

*TR variants: impact on Regional Parties*

Finally, the simulations for the 2015 Election indicate that TR adjustments to the existing constituency system would have had relatively little impact on the regional and local Parties. That too is what one would expect. These Parties contest seats only in the regions they serve. They do not have large numbers of unsuccessful votes across the country which might provide a basis for being allocated PMP seats. Their MPs would almost all be CMPs.

*Commentary*

The simulation results in Table 1 confirm how sensitive the outcomes in a TR-adjusted system would have been in 2015 to the chosen CMP / PMP ratios. This would be likely to be true in most years.

Certainly on this occasion, but probably on others as well, an 80:20 ratio with 130 or more PMP seats would (as already discussed) have produced a much more unsettled outcome than the other ratios involving fewer PMPs (perhaps 75 or thereabouts as illustrated).

The results also indicate that outcomes may be quite sensitive to the decision on whether to take surplus

83

successful votes into account as well as unsuccessful votes when allocating PMP seats to Parties.

When interpreting the results, one needs to bear in mind that the 2015 Election had some highly unusual features. The two traditionally dominant major Parties were both deeply split over the EU issue. No less significantly, there were *two* medium-size alternative Parties, UKIP and the Lib Dems, rather than the traditional *one*. Voters disenchanted with both of the major Parties probably supported the Lib Dems or UKIP according to their views on EU membership. So the UK's traditional "Third Party" vote was split two ways, thereby sharply reducing the number of seats that either Party won (as happens with a pure Constituency system) and allowing the Conservatives to win an overall majority. The extraordinary surge in support for UKIP, in particular, produced only one seat because their votes were widely distributed and not concentrated on particular constituencies.

Under a TR-adjusted electoral system, where every vote would have counted in some degree towards putting an MP in Parliament, voters would quite possibly have been less inclined in practice to vote for a Party such as UKIP whose policies other than its opposition to the EU were not well defined and whose survival prospects in the longer term seemed precarious.

## 2010 Election

Table 2 illustrates how combining the constituency system with TR might have affected the outcome of the 2010 Election. As in the simulations for 2015, the total number of MP seats is maintained in all cases at 650. So 326 seats were needed for an overall majority. These simulations too highlight some interesting points.

*Actual outcome (Table 2, column 1)*

On this earlier occasion, as is well known, no Party secured an overall majority. This was the unusual feature of the 2010 Election. The Conservative Party won 307 seats, 19 short of the number needed for an overall majority, but were able to take the important step (unfamiliar in recent UK experience) of forming a Coalition with the Lib Dems, who won 57 seats, thus securing a comfortable majority for the Coalition of 38 seats.

A Coalition of Labour (258 seats) and Lib Dems would have fallen 11 seats short of an overall majority and there is no obvious way that other Parties with this number of seats (or more) could have been persuaded to join the Coalition.

# Table 2

UK Election 2010
Seats actually won compared with simulations of seats won under pure PR and under TR (four variants)

| System | Actual FPTP | Pure PR | TR 80:20 UV only | TR 90:10 UV only | TR 88.5:11.5 UV only | UV+SSV |
|---|---|---|---|---|---|---|
| CMPs/PMPs | na | na | 520 /130 | 585/65 | 575/75 | 575 / 75 |
| | | | | | | |
| Cons | 307 | 235 | 274 | 290 | 288 | 295 |
| Lab | 258 | 189 | 236 | 247 | 245 | 248 |
| LD | 57 | 150 | 93 | 74 | 77 | 71 |
| UKIP | 0 | 20 | 8 | 4 | 5 | 3 |
| BNP | 0 | 12 | 5 | 2 | 3 | 2 |
| SNP | 6 | 11 | 8 | 7 | 7 | 7 |
| Green | 1 | 6 | 3 | 2 | 2 | 2 |
| SF | 5 | 4 | 5 | 6 | 5 | 5 |
| DUP | 8 | 4 | 7 | 7 | 7 | 7 |
| PC | 3 | 4 | 3 | 4 | 4 | 4 |
| SDLP | 3 | 2 | 3 | 3 | 3 | 3 |
| UCUNF | 0 | 2 | 1 | 1 | 1 | 0 |
| Eng Dem | 0 | 1 | 1 | 0 | 0 | 0 |
| Alliance | 1 | 1 | 1 | 1 | 1 | 1 |
| Independent | 1 | 0 | 1 | 1 | 1 | 1 |
| Others | 0 | 9 | 1 | 1 | 1 | 1 |
| | | | | | | |
| Totals: | 650 | 650 | 650 | 650 | 650 | 650 |

NOTES
- Total seats (CMPs+PMPs) are constrained to 650 in all TR cases so as to facilitate comparisons.
- For an overall majority, a Party (or Coalition) would have needed 326 seats or more.
- The Conservatives actually formed a Coalition with the LDs to obtain an overall majority (col 1) and could have done so again under any of the (simulated) systems in cols 2-6.
- With pure PR (col 2) either Cons or Lab could have formed a Coalition with the LDs.
- The TR variants in cols 3-5 allocate PMP seats to Parties in proportion to their shares in total *unsuccessful* votes cast (UV) only, based on CMP/PMP ratios of 80:20, 90:10 and 88.5:11.5. Seats won would have been sensitive to the ratios chosen. With an 80:20 ratio (col 3), but not the other ratios, a Lab+LD Coalition would have had a small overall majority.
- The col 6 TR variant allocates PMP seats to Parties in proportion to their shares in *unsuccessful plus surplus successful votes* (UV+ SSV), based on a CMP/PMP ratio of 88.5:11.5. Cons would have won 7 more seats but LDs 6 fewer seats.
- In all TR cases, medium-size Parties with national coverage (LDs especially but also UKIP and Greens) would have won more seats than they actually did.
- Regional Parties would have been little affected.
- Detailed supporting calculations are in Tables A3 and A4.

## Outcome with a pure PR system (column 2)

With a pure PR system (col 2 of Table 2), in which the proportions of seats allocated to individual Parties exactly matched their proportions of total votes cast across the country, the two largest Parties (Conservative & Labour) would each have been left with about 70 fewer seats than under the actual Constituency FPTP system. But the Liberal Democrats would have won 93 more seats and the smaller Parties with national coverage (UKIP, BNP and Greens) would likewise have won significant numbers of seats. The regional Parties, taken together, would have won a similar number of seats as under Constituency FPTP, though the SNP would have gained and the DUP would have lost several seats.

As under the actual Constituency FPTP system, therefore, a Coalition Government would have been inevitable under PR. In contrast with the actual outcome, however, both Conservatives and Labour would have been able to form a Coalition with the Lib Dems, and either Coalition would have commanded a substantial majority in Parliament without involving any of the other Parties. The Lib Dems would therefore have been king-makers, and protracted discussions between the potential Coalition Parties would have been likely.

## TR variants: impact on the major Parties

Under any of the TR variant specifications considered, the Conservatives with between 274 and 295 seats (as against the 307 they actually won) would again have needed, as they did under the present pure constituency system, to form a Coalition with the Lib Dems in order to secure an overall majority. In practice, *the two Parties would have been well able to do this. They could have formed the identical Coalition which they actually formed in 2010.* Under any of the TR variants this Coalition would have enjoyed comfortable majorities similar to the majority which they actually had between 2010 and 2015, though with rather fewer Conservative and rather more Lib Dem MPs.

*Under any of the three "realistic" TR variant specifications with smaller numbers of PMPs* (cols 4-6 of Table 2), *Labour would not have been able to form a Coalition with the Lib Dems alone* (any more than they could have done under the existing system) and would have struggled to form one with the Lib Dems and other Parties.

With an *80:20 CMP / PMP ratio, on the other hand, and 130 PMPs*, the position would have been more complicated. A Conservative / Lib Dem Coalition would still have commanded a comfortable majority overall. But a Coalition of Labour and the Lib Dems would also have had a majority overall (albeit a slim one of about 8 seats on an "unsuccessful votes only" basis and perhaps 2 seats on a "total wasted votes" basis) which they would not have had under the other TR specifications considered (and did not have under the present system). *The Lib Dems could in principle, therefore, have tried to form a precarious Coalition with Labour instead of the Conservatives.* They would in effect have been king-makers.

The simulations for this Election, therefore, likewise highlight *the risks of a more unsettled outcome if a TR ratio such as 80:20 with a large number of PMPs were chosen.*

*TR variants: comparative definitions of wasted votes*

In this 2010 Election, allocation of PMP seats on the basis of *total wasted votes* (surplus successful votes, SSV, as well as unsuccessful votes, UV) (compare cols 5 & 6 of Table 2) would again have benefited mainly the Conservative Party by giving them 7 more seats. More significantly, however, the Lib Dems would have lost 6 seats, thus probably putting a final nail in the coffin of a Labour / Lib Dem Coalition whose combined strength would have fallen by a further 3 seats. UKIP would have lost two, and BNP one, of their seats.

*TR variants:  impact on the medium-size Parties with wide national coverage*

With any of the CMP / PMP ratios considered, the medium-size Parties which attracted significant support *across the country* would have had significantly more representation in Parliament than they actually have under the present pure Constituency system.

The Lib Dems in particular would have had between 71 and 93 seats, depending on the TR specification chosen, rather than 57.

*Other medium-size Parties as well, however, would have gained some non-negligible representation in Parliament* through PMPs. UKIP and BNP would have had small numbers of seats (between 2 and 5 each) rather than none at all, and the Greens would have had 2 seats or 3 seats rather than one. The more PMPs there were, the more these Parties would have benefited. Their levels of representation would not, however, have enabled them to be spoilers or kingmakers.

*TR variants: impact on Regional Parties*

The regionally based parties in Scotland, Wales and Northern Ireland, on the other hand, would in 2010, as in 2015, mostly not have been much affected by a TR system, though the SNP would have won one or two more seats. The representation of these regionally-based Parties in Parliament would have continued to be predominantly via Constituency MPs.

*Commentary*

With a TR-adjusted system, therefore, the Conservatives would almost certainly have formed a Coalition with the Lib Dems after the 2010 Election, in the same way as actually happened.

Under any of the three "realistic" TR variants with smaller numbers of PMPs, Labour would have struggled to form a Coalition. Only the "unrealistic" 80:20 ratio coupled with allocation of PMP seats on a UV-only basis would in practical terms have opened the way to a credible Labour Coalition with the Lib Dems.

In all the cases considered, however, the Lib Dems and the other medium-size Parties would have won a fairer level of representation in the House of Commons.

When interpreting these results, one needs as previously noted to bear in mind that the 2010 Election too was unusual in its actual outcome, with neither of the two traditionally dominant Parties, Conservatives and Labour, obtaining an overall majority.

## Summary

In summary, then, and subject to the important qualification about voter behaviour discussed at the beginning of the Chapter, the main points which arise from the simulations for the contrasting ratios of CMPs to PMPs are as follows.

An 80:20 ratio, which would have brought as many as 130 PMPs into Parliament (and would bring in 150 with 600 MPs in total as proposed from 2018), does indeed feel, as earlier suggested, like a bridge too far. The simulations confirm that adding PMPs on this scale in the two Elections considered could have produced unsettled outcomes, posing a threat to stable and effective Government. In 2015, only the Conservatives could have led a Coalition, but they might well have struggled to win enough support from other Parties to provide an overall majority. In 2010, an 80:20 ratio, if combined with allocation of PMP seats on an unsuccessful-votes-only basis, would have produced a slim majority overall for a Labour / Lib Dem Coalition, and the Lib Dems could have tried as king-makers to form a Coalition with Labour instead of the Conservatives. In practice it seems highly unlikely that Parliament would have legislated in the first place for a ratio which would provide so many PMPs. We may therefore consider it unrealistic.

The ratios which would have brought 65 or 75 PMPs into Parliament, on the other hand, would appear to be entirely realistic and could seemingly have made valuable contributions to solving the problems of representation discussed earlier in the Chapter, without posing any threat to stable and effective government. The main simulated outcomes from these ratios are:

- Following the *2015 Election*, the Conservatives would not now have an overall, winner-takes-all majority in the House of Commons on the strength of their 37 per cent share of total votes cast but could have obtained an overall majority by forming a continuing Coalition with the Lib Dems (and if necessary another small Party). Labour could not in practice have led a Coalition.

- Following the *2010 Election*, the Conservatives and the Lib Dems would have been well able to form the identical Coalition which they actually formed under the present system. The Lib Dems might have been tempted to form a precarious Coalition with Labour and another Party rather than the Conservatives, but this would not have worked in practice with the 65 or 75 PMP variants.

- With PMP seats allocated on a *total wasted votes* basis, including surplus successful votes, the Conservatives would have obtained more seats in both Elections. They would still have needed to form Coalitions in order to secure overall majorities, but the task would have been easier.

- Following both Elections, the *medium-size and smaller Parties with national coverage* would have won significant levels of representation in Parliament, without posing a threat to stable and effective Government. With the partial exception of the Lib Dems, these Parties would depend primarily on PMP seats for obtaining representation in Parliament. The more PMP seats there are, therefore, the more seats these Parties would win.

- The SNP would have won one more seat in 2010 and half a dozen or so fewer seats in 2015, compared with the actual outcomes, but the other *regionally based Parties* in Wales and Northern Ireland would have shown little change compared with the present system. All these Parties would continue to depend predominantly on CMPs for their representation.

**General Lessons**

As already discussed more than once, both the latest Elections had unusual features, with neither of the two main Parties obtaining an outright majority in 2010 and UKIP attracting so many votes in 2015. Some caution is needed, therefore, when extrapolating from simulations for these two Elections to conclusions about Elections in general and future Elections in particular.

The simulations do confirm, however, that TR outcomes generally are likely to be sensitive to the choice of CMP / PMP ratios.

The more PMPs there are relative to CMPs, the closer the outcomes will be to those under proportional representation and the more challenging the formation of Coalitions (if needed) will tend to be. The more CMPs there are relative to PMPs, the closer the outcomes will be to those under the present Constituency FPTP system.

As discussed above, the simulations also indicate that in the last two Elections an 80:20 CMP / PMP ratio, with as many as 130 PMPs (or 150 PMPs with 600 constituencies), could in practice have posed a threat to stable and effective government. There is little doubt that a similar threat could occur on other occasions as well. This supports our instinct, discussed earlier, that such a ratio would probably be a bridge too far as well as being unlikely to be acceptable to Parliament. A TR specification providing for 75 PMPs or thereabouts would seem a far better place to begin and perhaps even to end.

There can similarly be little doubt that outcomes on future occasions may likewise be sensitive to the treatment of wasted votes, and in particular to whether surplus successful votes are taken into account as well as unsuccessful votes when allocating PMP seats to Parties.

Subject to these important points, and to the important qualifications discussed at the outset about induced changes in voter behaviour and the unusual features which were present in both Elections, the simulations give considerable support to *a priori* expectations that, with a TR-adjusted constituency system of the kind described including around 75 PMPs:

- Stable and effective government would continue to be possible.

- Coalition Governments could be somewhat more common, though not necessarily more so than single-Party Governments.

- By the same token, majority Governments able to govern without serious Parliamentary constraints could be somewhat less common, while doubtless continuing to be a familiar feature of the scene so long as there continue to be two dominant Parties.

- For the first time ever, medium-size Parties with national coverage would be likely to achieve respectable and defensible levels of representation in Parliament.

- For the first time ever, all voters would have some measure of representation in Parliament.

- For the first time ever, moreover, people throughout the country (and not just voters in marginal constituencies) would have a real incentive to vote and feel that their vote mattered.

**Coalition Governments in perspective**

Since Coalition Governments might occur rather more often under a TR-adjusted constituency system, it is pertinent to consider the pros and cons of such Governments and the wider implications.

Many people in our country instinctively view Coalition Governments with suspicion and distaste, preferring to elect a stable Government which can govern without major constraints or hindrances in Parliament. There is a lingering conventional wisdom which associates Coalition

Governments with instability and weak government. The difficulties which countries such as Israel and The Netherlands experience in forming and re-forming Coalitions, and in providing firm, stable government, are often seen as a terrible indictment of Coalitions, and people with perceptions and concerns such as these may quite understandably see the increased likelihood of Coalition Governments as a disadvantage of the TR system.

The fact is, however, that there are good Coalitions and troublesome Coalitions. Troublesome Coalitions are typically found in countries whose electoral systems are based on pure versions of proportional representation (PR). Such systems notoriously encourage a proliferation of small Parties, often with extreme views, which are able to wield influence out of all proportion to the level of popular support they command.

A TR-adjusted Constituency system with a limited number of PMPs, by contrast, would not be remotely like a pure PR system. It would preserve the precious traditional system of Constituency MPs, elected on a FPTP basis, but supplement it with the small but significant addition of some Party MPs, elected on a basis closer to proportional representation but still personally elected as individuals, so as to remove (or at least soften) the most troublesome, unreasonable, divisive and least defensible consequences (none of them intended) of an exclusively Constituency FPTP system.

There is no denying that periods when Coalition Governments are being formed may be demanding and unsettling. There is also, however, much experience to suggest that such Governments can be seriously beneficial as well, not least in promoting policies which command wide public support and restraining the largest Parties from putting their own agenda and prejudices ahead of proceeding in accordance with a broader national consensus. Countries where Coalitions are more frequent may also have less tendency to lurch from one extreme of policy to another when Governments change.

If one looks at experience elsewhere, there is little doubt that many countries whose electoral systems include degrees of proportionality are able to deliver stable and effective government. A non-political Ministry of Justice Study in 2007 found it is hard to detect any difference, in terms of stability and effective government, between FPTP systems and systems employing proportionality.

For all these reasons, it is easy to exaggerate concerns about stability and governability in the kind of Coalition Governments which a TR-adjusted system might encourage in the UK, provided that the number of PMPs remains relatively small. There are no solid grounds for concluding that such Coalitions, somewhat more frequent as they would probably be, would make the country ungovernable or give smaller Parties a stranglehold influence out of proportion to their support in the country. Coalition Governments resulting from TR-based elections would be much more likely to resemble those which the UK had between 2010 and 2015 and during World War Two rather than the kind of Governments sometimes seen in countries using extreme versions of PR.

In present circumstances, moreover, some at least of the Coalition Governments which might have been formed in

2015 would arguably have been able to serve the country at least as well as the Conservatives on their own have succeeded in doing. There seems a good chance, for example, that the issue of future relationships with the EU and the Referendum would have been as well or even (dare one say?) better handled by a Coalition Government including Lib Dems than by David Cameron's single-Party Government.

On the other side of the argument, our present system is letting down many, or even most, of the electorate, virtually disenfranchising them. Focussing again on the 2015 outcome, it is far from easy to justify a system in which:

- A Party supported by only 37 per cent of voters (and less than 25 percent of the electorate) now has an absolute majority and claims a national mandate even though 63 per cent of voters voted for others.
- Even moderate-size Parties struggle to win any representation at all: UKIP, the Lib Dems and the Greens currently have only 10 seats between them despite polling 7½ million votes (not far short of Labour's 9.3 million).
- Many of the electorate do not even vote (turnout rates seldom reach two-thirds of the electorate) and receive no representation if they do.
- Only in a limited number of marginal constituencies do individual voters have any strong incentive to vote at all.
- Many, if not most, of the votes which voters do cast are unlikely to have any effect on the outcome.

A Constituency system with even small TR additions at the margin could do much to alleviate these troublesome features by giving a much more defensible level of representation to millions of voters. If we again look at the 2015 Election, a system such as that specified in column 6 of Table 1, with 75 PMPs allocated to Parties on a total wasted votes basis (UVs + SSVs), would have given a limited but reasonable voice inside Parliament to Parties which are now manifestly under-represented in relation to the number of their supporters, notably UKIP, the Lib Dems, and the Green Party:

- UKIP, with nearly 4 million votes, would have had 14 MPs rather than one.
- The Lib-Dems, with nearly 2½ million votes, would have had 15 MPs rather than 8,
- The Green Party, with more than a million votes, would have had 5 MPs rather than one.

In terms of social cohesion and a successful country, it is asking for trouble to deny an effective voice within Parliament to these and other shades of opinion. When people feel that they cannot make their voices heard, they are likely to become dissidents and demonstrators in Trafalgar Square (and of course in town squares across the country). The better course must surely be to encourage such people, as a constituency system with limited TR additions would do, to bring their cases to Westminster and put their reasoned arguments forward in the principal Chamber of the Mother of Parliaments.

## TABLE A1

## Simulations of Total Representation (TR) in the UK General Election, May 2015

Actual outcomes compared with TR simulations for CMP/PMP ratios of 80:20 and 90:10,
PMP seats being allocated to Parties in proportion to their shares in total unsuccessful votes only

| Party | Actual Election Results | | | | TR outcomes with 80:20 ratio (520 CMPs / 130 PMPs) | | | | | | | TR outcomes with 90:10 ratio (585 CMPs / 65 PMPs) | | | | | |
|---|---|---|---|---|---|---|---|---|---|---|---|---|---|---|---|---|---|
| | Votes Cast | | Seats | | Adjusted CMPs | Successful Votes | Unsuccessful Votes | | PMPs 130 | Total Seats | | Adjusted CMPs | Unsuccessful Votes | | PMPs 65 | Total Seats | |
| C | 11,334,920 | 36.92% | 331 | 50.92% | 265 | 8,392,085 | 2,942,835 | 19.10% | 25 | 290 | 44.62% | 298 | 2,942,835 | 19.10% | 13 | 311 | 47.85% |
| Lab | 9,347,326 | 30.45% | 232 | 35.69% | 186 | 5,013,580 | 4,333,746 | 28.12% | 37 | 223 | 34.31% | 208 | 4,333,746 | 28.12% | 18 | 226 | 34.77% |
| UKIP | 3,881,129 | 12.64% | 1 | 0.15% | 1 | 19,642 | 3,861,487 | 25.06% | 33 | 34 | 5.23% | 1 | 3,861,487 | 25.06% | 16 | 17 | 2.62% |
| LD | 2,415,888 | 7.87% | 8 | 1.23% | 6 | 135,732 | 2,280,156 | 14.80% | 19 | 25 | 3.85% | 7 | 2,280,156 | 14.80% | 10 | 17 | 2.62% |
| SNP | 1,454,436 | 4.74% | 56 | 8.62% | 45 | 1,409,229 | 45,207 | 0.29% | 0 | 45 | 6.92% | 50 | 45,207 | 0.29% | 0 | 50 | 7.69% |
| Green | 1,157,613 | 3.77% | 1 | 0.15% | 1 | 22,871 | 1,134,742 | 7.36% | 10 | 11 | 1.69% | 1 | 1,134,742 | 7.36% | 5 | 6 | 0.92% |
| DUP | 184,260 | 0.60% | 8 | 1.23% | 6 | 133,082 | 51,178 | 0.33% | 1 | 7 | 1.08% | 7 | 51,178 | 0.33% | 0 | 7 | 1.08% |
| PC | 181,694 | 0.59% | 3 | 0.46% | 2 | 38,741 | 142,953 | 0.93% | 1 | 3 | 0.46% | 3 | 142,953 | 0.93% | 1 | 4 | 0.62% |
| SF | 176,232 | 0.57% | 4 | 0.62% | 3 | 76,393 | 99,839 | 0.65% | 1 | 4 | 0.62% | 4 | 99,839 | 0.65% | 1 | 5 | 0.77% |
| UUP | 114,935 | 0.37% | 2 | 0.31% | 2 | 35,550 | 79,385 | 0.52% | 1 | 3 | 0.46% | 2 | 79,385 | 0.52% | 0 | 2 | 0.31% |
| SDLP | 99,809 | 0.33% | 3 | 0.46% | 2 | 45,362 | 54,447 | 0.35% | 1 | 3 | 0.46% | 3 | 54,447 | 0.35% | 0 | 3 | 0.46% |
| Indep | 17,689 | 0.06% | 1 | 0.15% | 1 | 17,689 | 0 | 0.00% | 0 | 1 | 0.15% | 1 | 0 | 0.00% | 0 | 1 | 0.15% |
| Others | 332,279 | 1.08% | 0 | 0.00% | 0 | 0 | 384,585 | 2.50% | 1 | 1 | 0.15% | 0 | 384,585 | 2.50% | 1 | 1 | 0.15% |
| Totals: | 30,698,210 | 100.00% | 650 | 100.00% | 520 | 15,339,956 | 15,410,560 | 100.00% | 130 | 650 | 100.00% | 585 | 15,410,560 | 100.00% | 65 | 650 | 100.00% |

NOTES
Adjusted CMP numbers for the Parties in the simulated TR outcomes are calculated as 80% and 90%
of the seats they actually won, suitably rounded, so as to keep 650 MPs in total.
The Speaker's seat is included in votes cast for, and seats won by, the Conservatives.

## TABLE A2

**Further simulations of Total Representation (TR) in the UK General Election, May 2015**
Variant TR outcomes, with & without crediting of surplus successful votes, both based on 575 CMPs & 75 PMPs, compared with Actual FPTP and pure PR outcomes

| Party | Actual Election Results (Constituency FPTP) | | | Pure PR outcome | TR outcomes with 88.5:11.5 ratio (575 CMPs / 75 PMPs), and taking account of: surplus successful votes as well as unsuccessful votes | | | | | | | | | unsuccessful votes only | | | | | |
|---|---|---|---|---|---|---|---|---|---|---|---|---|---|---|---|---|---|---|---|
| | Votes Cast | | Seats | Seats | Adjusted CMP nos | Successful Votes | Unsuccessful Votes | Surplus successful votes | Unsuccessful plus Surplus votes | | PMPs 75 | Total Seats | | Adjusted CMP nos | Unsuccessful Votes | | PMPs 75 | Total Seats | |
| C | 11,334,920 | 36.92% | 331 | 240 | 293 | 8,392,085 | 2,942,835 | 4,290,261 | 7,233,096 | 31.64% | 24 | 317 | 48.73% | 293 | 2,942,835 | 19.10% | 14 | 307 | 47.23% |
| Lab | 9,347,326 | 30.45% | 232 | 198 | 205 | 5,013,580 | 4,333,746 | 2,428,841 | 6,762,587 | 29.58% | 22 | 227 | 34.92% | 205 | 4,333,746 | 28.12% | 21 | 226 | 34.77% |
| UKIP | 3,881,129 | 12.64% | 1 | 82 | 1 | 19,642 | 3,861,487 | 3,437 | 3,864,924 | 16.91% | 13 | 14 | 2.10% | 1 | 3,861,487 | 25.06% | 19 | 20 | 3.08% |
| LD | 2,415,888 | 7.87% | 8 | 51 | 7 | 135,732 | 2,280,156 | 24,968 | 2,305,124 | 10.08% | 8 | 15 | 2.24% | 7 | 2,280,156 | 14.80% | 11 | 18 | 2.77% |
| SNP | 1,454,436 | 4.74% | 56 | 31 | 49 | 1,409,229 | 45,207 | 558,097 | 603,304 | 2.64% | 2 | 51 | 7.85% | 49 | 45,207 | 0.29% | 0 | 49 | 7.54% |
| Green | 1,157,613 | 3.77% | 1 | 25 | 1 | 22,871 | 1,134,742 | 7,967 | 1,142,709 | 5.00% | 4 | 5 | 0.73% | 1 | 1,134,742 | 7.36% | 6 | 7 | 1.08% |
| DUP | 184,260 | 0.60% | 8 | 4 | 7 | 133,082 | 51,178 | 58,517 | 109,695 | 0.48% | 0 | 7 | 1.13% | 7 | 51,178 | 0.33% | 0 | 7 | 1.08% |
| PC | 181,694 | 0.59% | 3 | 4 | 3 | 38,741 | 142,953 | 14,528 | 157,481 | 0.69% | 0 | 4 | 0.62% | 3 | 142,953 | 0.93% | 1 | 4 | 0.62% |
| SF | 176,232 | 0.57% | 4 | 4 | 3 | 76,393 | 99,839 | 40,218 | 140,057 | 0.61% | 0 | 3 | 0.53% | 3 | 99,839 | 0.65% | 1 | 4 | 0.62% |
| UUP | 114,935 | 0.37% | 2 | 2 | 2 | 35,550 | 79,385 | 1,479 | 80,864 | 0.35% | 0 | 2 | 0.35% | 2 | 79,385 | 0.52% | 1 | 3 | 0.46% |
| SDLP | 99,809 | 0.33% | 3 | 2 | 3 | 45,362 | 54,447 | 12,843 | 67,290 | 0.29% | 0 | 3 | 0.50% | 3 | 54,447 | 0.35% | 0 | 3 | 0.46% |
| Indep | 17,689 | 0.06% | 1 | 0 | 1 | 17,689 | 0 | 9,202 | 9,202 | 0.04% | 0 | 1 | 0.16% | 1 | 0 | 0.00% | 0 | 1 | 0.15% |
| Others | 332,279 | 1.08% | 0 | 7 | 0 | 0 | 384,585 | 0 | 384,585 | 1.68% | 1 | 1 | 0.19% | 0 | 384,585 | 2.50% | 1 | 1 | 0.15% |
| **Totals:** | **30,698,210** | **100.00%** | **650** | **650** | **575** | **15,339,956** | **15,410,560** | **7,450,358** | **22,860,918** | **100.00%** | **75** | **650** | **100.00%** | **575** | **15,410,560** | **100.00%** | **75** | **650** | **100.00%** |

NOTES
Adjusted CMP numbers for the Parties in the simulated TR outcomes are calculated as 88.5% of the seats they actually won, suitably rounded, so as to keep 650 MPs in total.
The Speaker's seat is included in the the votes cast for, and seats won by, the Conservatives.

**TABLE A3**

## Simulations of Total Representation (TR) in the UK General Election, May 2010

Actual outcomes compared with TR simulations for CMP/PMP ratios of 80:20 and 90:10,
PMP seats being allocated to Parties in proportion to their shares in total unsuccessful votes only

| | Actual Election Results | | | | TR outcomes with 80:20 ratio (520 CMPs / 130 PMPs) | | | | | | | TR outcomes with 90:10 ratio (585 CMPs / 65 PMPs) | | | | | |
|---|---|---|---|---|---|---|---|---|---|---|---|---|---|---|---|---|---|
| Party | Votes Cast | | Seats | | Adjusted CMP nos | Successful Votes | Unsuccessful Votes | | PMPs 130 | Total Seats | | Adjusted CMP nos | Unsuccessful Votes | | PMPs 65 | Total Seats | |
| C | 10,706,388 | 36.11% | 307 | 47.23% | 246 | 7,302,080 | 3,404,308 | 21.73% | 28 | 274 | 42.15% | 276 | 3,404,308 | 21.73% | 14 | 290 | 44.62% |
| Lab | 8,601,349 | 29.01% | 258 | 39.69% | 206 | 5,000,922 | 3,600,427 | 22.98% | 30 | 236 | 36.31% | 232 | 3,600,427 | 22.98% | 15 | 247 | 38.00% |
| LD | 6,827,832 | 23.03% | 57 | 8.77% | 46 | 1,231,743 | 5,596,089 | 35.72% | 47 | 93 | 14.31% | 51 | 5,596,089 | 35.72% | 23 | 74 | 11.38% |
| UKIP | 917,175 | 3.09% | 0 | 0.00% | 0 | 0 | 917,175 | 5.85% | 8 | 8 | 1.23% | 0 | 917,175 | 5.85% | 4 | 4 | 0.62% |
| BNP | 564,321 | 1.90% | 0 | 0.00% | 0 | 0 | 564,321 | 3.60% | 5 | 5 | 0.77% | 0 | 564,321 | 3.60% | 2 | 2 | 0.31% |
| SNP | 491,376 | 1.66% | 6 | 0.92% | 5 | 88,352 | 403,024 | 2.57% | 3 | 8 | 1.23% | 5 | 403,024 | 2.57% | 2 | 7 | 1.08% |
| Green | 285,616 | 0.96% | 1 | 0.15% | 1 | 16,238 | 269,378 | 1.72% | 2 | 3 | 0.46% | 1 | 269,378 | 1.72% | 1 | 2 | 0.31% |
| SF | 171,942 | 0.58% | 5 | 0.77% | 4 | 102,290 | 69,652 | 0.44% | 1 | 5 | 0.77% | 5 | 69,652 | 0.44% | 1 | 6 | 0.92% |
| DUP | 168,216 | 0.57% | 8 | 1.23% | 6 | 119,235 | 48,981 | 0.31% | 1 | 7 | 1.08% | 7 | 48,981 | 0.31% | 0 | 7 | 1.08% |
| PC | 165,394 | 0.56% | 3 | 0.46% | 2 | 35,743 | 129,651 | 0.83% | 1 | 3 | 0.46% | 3 | 129,651 | 0.83% | 1 | 4 | 0.62% |
| SDLP | 110,970 | 0.37% | 3 | 0.46% | 2 | 51,596 | 59,374 | 0.38% | 1 | 3 | 0.46% | 3 | 59,374 | 0.38% | 0 | 3 | 0.46% |
| UCUNF | 102,361 | 0.35% | 0 | 0.00% | 0 | 0 | 102,361 | 0.65% | 1 | 1 | 0.15% | 0 | 102,361 | 0.65% | 1 | 1 | 0.15% |
| Eng Dem | 64,826 | 0.22% | 0 | 0.00% | 0 | 0 | 64,826 | 0.41% | 1 | 1 | 0.15% | 0 | 64,826 | 0.41% | 0 | 0 | 0.00% |
| Alliance | 42,762 | 0.14% | 1 | 0.15% | 1 | 12,839 | 29,923 | 0.19% | 0 | 1 | 0.15% | 1 | 29,923 | 0.19% | 0 | 1 | 0.15% |
| Independ | 21,181 | 0.07% | 1 | 0.15% | 1 | 21,181 | 0 | 0.00% | 0 | 1 | 0.15% | 1 | 0 | 0.00% | 0 | 1 | 0.15% |
| Others | 408,502 | 1.38% | 0 | 0.00% | 0 | 0 | 408,502 | 2.61% | 1 | 1 | 0.15% | 0 | 408,502 | 2.61% | 1 | 1 | 0.15% |
| Totals: | 29,650,211 | 100.00% | 650 | 100.00% | 520 | 13,982,219 | 15,667,992 | 100.00% | 130 | 650 | 100.00% | 585 | 15,667,992 | 100.00% | 65 | 650 | 100.00% |

NOTES

Adjusted CMP numbers for the Parties in the simulated TR outcomes are calculated as 80% and 90%
of the seats they actually won, suitably rounded, so as to keep 650 MPs in total.
The Speaker's seat is included in votes cast for, and seats won by, the Conservatives.

## TABLE A4

### Further simulations of Total Representation (TR) in the UK General Election, May 2010

Variant TR outcomes, with & without crediting of surplus successful votes, both based on 575 CMPs & 75 PMPs, compared with Actual FPTP and pure PR outcomes

| Party | Actual Election Results (Constituency FPTP) Votes Cast | | Seats | | Pure PR Outcome Seats | TR outcomes with 88.5:11.5 ratio (575 CMPs / 75 PMPs), and taking account of: surplus successful votes as well as unsuccessful votes Adjusted CMP nos | Successful Votes | Unsuccessful Votes | Surplus successful votes | Unsuccessful plus Surplus votes | | PMPs 75 | Total Seats | | unsuccessful votes only Adjusted CMP nos | PMPs 75 | Total Seats | |
|---|---|---|---|---|---|---|---|---|---|---|---|---|---|---|---|---|---|---|
| C | 10,706,388 | 36.11% | 307 | 47.23% | 235 | 272 | 7,302,080 | 3,404,308 | 2,901,945 | 6,306,253 | 29.91% | 23 | 295 | 45.38% | 272 | 16 | 288 | 44.31% |
| Lab | 8,601,349 | 29.01% | 258 | 39.69% | 189 | 228 | 5,000,922 | 3,600,427 | 2,040,113 | 5,640,540 | 26.75% | 20 | 248 | 38.15% | 228 | 17 | 245 | 37.69% |
| LD | 6,827,832 | 23.03% | 57 | 8.77% | 150 | 50 | 1,231,743 | 5,596,089 | 315,947 | 5,912,036 | 28.04% | 21 | 71 | 10.92% | 50 | 27 | 77 | 11.85% |
| UKIP | 917,175 | 3.09% | 0 | 0.00% | 20 | 0 | 0 | 917,175 | 0 | 917,175 | 4.35% | 3 | 3 | 0.46% | 0 | 5 | 5 | 0.77% |
| BNP | 564,321 | 1.90% | 0 | 0.00% | 12 | 0 | 0 | 564,321 | 0 | 564,321 | 2.68% | 2 | 2 | 0.31% | 0 | 3 | 3 | 0.46% |
| SNP | 491,376 | 1.66% | 6 | 0.92% | 11 | 5 | 88,352 | 403,024 | 20,984 | 424,008 | 2.01% | 2 | 7 | 1.08% | 5 | 2 | 7 | 1.08% |
| Green | 285,616 | 0.96% | 1 | 0.15% | 6 | 1 | 16,238 | 269,378 | 1,252 | 270,630 | 1.28% | 1 | 2 | 0.31% | 1 | 1 | 2 | 0.31% |
| SF | 171,942 | 0.58% | 5 | 0.77% | 4 | 4 | 102,290 | 69,652 | 41,280 | 110,932 | 0.53% | 1 | 5 | 0.77% | 4 | 1 | 5 | 0.77% |
| DUP | 168,216 | 0.57% | 8 | 1.23% | 4 | 7 | 119,235 | 48,981 | 47,813 | 96,794 | 0.46% | 0 | 7 | 1.08% | 7 | 0 | 7 | 1.08% |
| PC | 165,394 | 0.56% | 3 | 0.46% | 4 | 3 | 35,743 | 129,651 | 11,303 | 140,954 | 0.67% | 1 | 4 | 0.62% | 3 | 1 | 4 | 0.62% |
| SDLP | 110,970 | 0.37% | 3 | 0.46% | 2 | 3 | 51,596 | 59,374 | 19,162 | 78,536 | 0.37% | 0 | 3 | 0.46% | 3 | 0 | 3 | 0.46% |
| UCUNF | 102,361 | 0.35% | 0 | 0.00% | 2 | 0 | 0 | 102,361 | 0 | 102,361 | 0.49% | 0 | 0 | 0.00% | 0 | 1 | 1 | 0.15% |
| Eng Dem | 64,826 | 0.22% | 0 | 0.00% | 1 | 0 | 0 | 64,826 | 0 | 64,826 | 0.31% | 0 | 0 | 0.00% | 0 | 0 | 0 | 0.00% |
| Alliance | 42,762 | 0.14% | 1 | 0.15% | 1 | 1 | 12,839 | 29,923 | 1,533 | 31,456 | 0.15% | 0 | 1 | 0.15% | 1 | 0 | 1 | 0.15% |
| Independ | 21,181 | 0.07% | 1 | 0.15% | 0 | 1 | 21,181 | 0 | 14,364 | 14,364 | 0.07% | 0 | 1 | 0.15% | 1 | 0 | 1 | 0.15% |
| Others | 408,502 | 1.38% | 0 | 0.00% | 9 | 0 | 0 | 408,502 | 0 | 408,502 | 1.94% | 1 | 1 | 0.15% | 0 | 1 | 1 | 0.15% |
| Totals: | 29,650,211 | 100.00% | 650 | 100.00% | 650 | 575 | 13,982,219 | 15,667,992 | 5,415,696 | 21,083,688 | 100.00% | 75 | 650 | 100.00% | 575 | 75 | 650 | 100.00% |

NOTES

Adjusted CMP numbers for the Parties in the simulated TR outcomes are calculated as 88.5% of the seats they actually won, suitably rounded, so as to keep 650 MPs in total.

The Speaker's seat is included in the the votes cast for, and seats won by, the Conservatives.

# Chapter 4
*by Aharon Nathan*

## HOUSE OF LORDS REFORM, INCLUDING A TR ELECTORAL SYSTEM

### Introduction

This Chapter sets out our thoughts on the much-visited subject of how best to reform the House of Lords, with special reference to the role which the principle of Total Representation (TR) might play in electing members of the reformed House.

### The need for a second Chamber

The first question, clearly, is: do we need a second chamber? The answer is, I suggest, an emphatic Yes.

The purpose of the House of Commons, as representatives of the people, all the people, is to legislate by proxy on their behalf and supervise the State's Executive branch, the Government. As the House of Commons has evolved in the last hundred years, however, it has become dominated by political Parties which are too often willing to put Party interests above national priorities. The Parties, with their Whips, have come to dominate the House of Commons, pushing it into constant adversarial confrontations, and the Legislature, and first arm of State, has become subordinated in large measure to the Executive, the Government.

These unwelcome developments have made the case for having a second Chamber more compelling than ever.

Like many others, therefore, I believe that the House of Lords, suitably reformed, has a continuing and important role to play as a second, independent Revising Chamber which can ask the House of Commons to think again and has the power to delay, but not ultimately to frustrate, decisions of the House of Commons.

## An elected second Chamber

To fulfill this role, and indeed to be genuinely part of a democratic Parliament at all, the House of Lords needs to represent the people, and therefore to be an elected House. A non-elected Parliament is almost a contradiction in terms. As Lord Strathclyde, then Leader of the Opposition in the Lords, wrote to me in a letter of 25th November 2003,

> *"For my part, I have a simple view. I think that in the 21st Century the political members of a House of Parliament should be elected directly by the people."*

On 4th October 2004 Lord Falconer, then Secretary of State and Lord Chancellor wrote to me :

> *"The Government's aim is to create a second chamber which fulfills a very important role within Parliament, as a revising chamber for legislation and as a body made representative of the nation."*

The reformed House should therefore not, I suggest, be made up of unelected hereditary peers and other peers whom Governments can appoint in order to assure themselves of a majority, thus frustrating the main purpose of such a House. Continuing to appoint Lords in this way, so as to duplicate the Commons, is bringing the House of Lords into dysfunction and eventually into disrepute.

Neither, in my opinion, should members of the reformed House of Lords be entitled to remain members throughout their lives.

I believe, on the contrary, that members of the House should be elected by the people for fixed terms of years, perhaps six years, with sensitive arrangements for transition from the present membership.

As with the House of Commons, I would see considerable merit in using a system which combines Constituencies with Total Representation (TR) for electing members of the reformed House. Apart from being a good system in itself this would help to restore the long-lost link between the Lords and the electorate across the country.

The electoral system and other arrangements should be developed so as to provide maximum assurance that the reformed House does not become a replica of the House of Commons or another rubber-stamping subordinate of the Government of the day.

Later sections of this Chapter will return to these points.

## Functions

I assume that a new Act of Reform would broadly confirm the existing functions of the House of Lords, as defined in the Parliament Acts of 1911 and 1949, including its power to propose changes to most legislation and delay its passage but not ultimately to frustrate the will of the Commons.

## Membership

As already suggested, the reformed House of Lords would consist entirely of members elected by the people for fixed terms of years, and representing the people who have elected them, with sensitive arrangements for transition from the present membership.

Some commentators argue that we need to retain some appointed Lords to ensure the presence of experts. In my opinion, this is a spurious argument. The House of Lords was never intended to be a House of experts. Governments and Select Committees of both Houses can and frequently do draw on expert advice from outside. Parliaments exist democratically to represent the ordinary citizen, not to create oligarchies and establishments that further distance the representatives from the represented.

There are, however, two categories of people who have traditionally been members of the House of Lords and whose special status could if desired, be recognised, with suitable modifications, within the new arrangements. These are: Law Lords and Bishops.

The challenge would be to give these dignitaries, few in number, a special status within the new chamber without doing violence to the Montesquieu principle of separation of powers between the three arms of State – Legislature, Executive and Judiciary – and without sacrificing the principle that the new House of Lords should consist entirely of elected members.

The solution could lie in providing for a number of non-voting Judicial and Religious Assessors who would be allowed to participate actively in the deliberations of the new House of Lords and its Committees but would not have the right to vote.

The Judicial Assessors would preferably be members of the Judiciary with real and current Bench experience, so that a direct link between the sovereign people and the judiciary would be maintained. The Supreme Court might delegate a small number of judges from the practising Judiciary to sit in the Lords on this basis and contribute as appropriate to its deliberations for a certain limited period – say six years. After these six years, they would be rotated and replaced by others.

Similarly with Bishops and / or other religious leaders, the Queen as Sovereign could appoint a small number of these to sit as Assessors in the new House on a similar, non-voting basis, again for a period of six years, after which they too would be rotated.

Arrangements on these lines, though by no means essential, could neatly solve the problem of how to replace the Law Lords and Bishops, thus maintaining the *gravitas* of the second Chamber. Such arrangements could also help in the vital task of restoring social cohesion in the UK, which has been threatened by social and ideological trends from within and as a result of an unprecedented scale of immigration from without.

I would also see advantage in continuing to have within the House of Lords people with long experience of important areas of the public and private sectors.

The House of Commons now includes many young people who look at their membership of Parliament as a career. They have become professional MPs. In my opinion, however, membership of Parliament should not be a profession. The recent development of this practice has contributed to the chasm between citizens and the MPs they elect to represent them, who look at their membership as a job for life. It is only the enterprising among them who move on and use their parliamentary positions as launching-pads to go forward into other careers, often more remunerative or more rewarding, in business, journalism or academia.

To avoid creating a similar problem in the new House of Lords, and to balance the two Houses as to age and experience, I would see a case for fixing the minimum age of members of the Lords at 40. This would help in attracting individuals with wide experience from a variety of backgrounds, some of whom at least would have already made their mark or their fortune and so would be able to devote the mature years of their lives to public service rather than building up new careers elsewhere.

There may also be a case for limiting the service of individual members of the reformed House of Lords to three or four six-year periods and introducing an upper age-limit of 75 or 80. This could help the new House to maintain its vitality and avoid inertia.

**Elections to the new Chamber**

As discussed earlier, I believe that a system combining Constituencies with Total Representation (TR) would work well for electing members of the reformed House of Lords as well as the House of Commons. How might such a system be applied in practice to the Lords?

Here, as in the Commons, there would be a range of options. My suggestions would be as follows. The numbers should be seen as an illustrative guide, and not set in stone.

- The new House of Lords could have (say) 300 members.

- 200 of these could be Regional Lords (RLs), elected like Constituency MPs through a Constituency FPTP system, region by region.

- Each House of Lords Constituency or Electoral Region would consist of three contiguous constituencies out of the 600 House of Commons constituencies due to be introduced from 2018. This would remove the need for a whole new exercise by the Boundary Commissions to determine Lords Regions and would vastly simplify the ongoing tasks of organisation and administration. The UK already has far too many conflicting administrative geographies and boundaries which are a major source of waste and inefficiency.

- The remaining Members of the reformed Chamber (up to, say, 100) would be Party Lords (PLs). It would be a matter for decision how many of these there should be. If the chosen number were 100, that would mean a ratio of Regional to Party Lords of 67:33. The proportion of Party Lords would then be higher than those discussed earlier for Party MPs in the Commons,

111

thereby giving a significantly higher weighting than in the Commons to "wasted" votes. This might, however, be considered appropriate for a more independent second Chamber with less Party whipping (see further below). It would significantly reduce the likelihood that any single Party in the reformed House of Lords would have an overall majority. It might also correct to some extent for the relatively low weighting of Party MPs (PMPs) envisaged for the Commons.

- As in the House of Commons, Party Lord quotas of seats would be allocated to individual Parties in proportion to their shares in the aggregate of "wasted" votes they had obtained, and the Party quotas of seats would then be allocated to the individual candidates within each Party who had personally won most seats in the election, in the same way as described for Party MPs in Chapter 2. The "wasted" votes ought preferably to be defined to include surplus votes obtained by successful RL candidates as well as votes for unsuccessful candidates so as to make the overall balance of Lords more closely correspond to (and represent) the overall balance of voters in the country.

## Provision for Independent or Cross-Bench Lords

Independent or "cross-bench" Peers have traditionally contributed much to the work of the House of Lords. It would be good to enable this tradition to continue.

To that end, I would hope that Parliament might agree to strengthen and codify an existing, un-codified tradition whereby all members of the House of Lords, whatever the Party banner may be under which they have been elected, are encouraged to assume a degree of independence, seeing their main allegiance as being to Queen (in accordance with the oath sworn by Members of both Houses of Parliament and the more recent House of Lords Code of Conduct) and acting in case of need according to their own consciences and judgments of the public interest rather than following Party lines. The Office of Party Whip should preferably be abolished, as should the central aisle, so as to convey that all members, once elected, become "cross-benchers" first and foremost.

Whether or not that can be achieved, one consequence which may still be seen as regrettable of an electoral system on the lines proposed, is that independent or "cross-bench" candidates who wish as a matter of principle to forswear affiliation or allegiance to any of the political Parties, would have a lesser chance of being elected than candidates who are so affiliated. Such candidates might include aspiring people with professional backgrounds or experience who could bring much value to the House.

Candidates of this kind, though they would lack the back-up support which Parties may provide, would in other respects have a similar chance with Party-affiliated candidates of being elected as *Regional* Lords, especially if there was a good public understanding of the different natures of the two Houses. They could stand in the regions as Independent Candidates.

Other things being equal, however, they would have no chance of winning seats as *Party* Lords when the "wasted" votes are allocated to Parties. So the electoral system could be seen as being biased against potentially excellent candidates who wish to forswear *any* Party affiliation or allegiance.

It might be necessary to accept this as being a consequence of having an elected House with good representation of the people.

Candidates wishing to run as independents could, however, improve their chances of winning Party Lord seats by teaming up or forming pre-alliances with other like-minded independents. Alternatively, they might be able to form a "strictly non-partisan" Party exclusively consisting of candidates who wish to forswear affiliation or allegiance to any of the political Parties and are committed to act and vote individually according to their consciences and perceptions of the public interest, drawing on their professional expertise and experience. That would be the Party's (sole) declared policy and position. Such a Party could even prove to be a significant force in the reformed House of Lords as well as helping the new House to attract professional candidates similar to those who have contributed so much as cross-benchers in the present House.

## Constituency sizes and responsibilities

As already implied, an electoral system for the reformed House of Lords which combines Constituency and TR elements would require regions or constituencies to be defined.

Under the proposals already discussed, the reformed House would have only one-third as many Regional or Constituency Lords as there would be Constituency MPs

114

in the Commons, representing only one-third as many regions or constituencies. Each House of Lords region or constituency would comprise three House of Commons constituencies.

This would not, I believe, be a problem but rather a strength of the new system. Regional Lords would not have the same obligations which Constituency MPs have to maintain close contact at all time with their constituencies. They would not be obliged to set up "surgeries" similar to those of Constituency MPs. Their contacts would be more a matter of gauging the political temperatures of their regions and using these to inform the deliberations of the House. The roles of MPs and Lords would complement, rather than duplicate, each other. This in itself would add to the value of the Lords as a Revising Chamber.

## Frequency of elections

As suggested earlier, members of the reformed House of Lords could be elected for terms of six years. Once the new system is up and running, elections for the whole House could take place every six years. This period would be fixed. Alternatively, elections for half the members could take place every three years. This period too would be fixed. In contrast with the Commons, the House of Lords would not be able to dissolve itself.

## By-elections

If a Regional Lord dies or resigns, a by-election would be initiated and moved by an appropriate House Committee within two months of the death or resignation of the Lord concerned.

If a Party Lord dies or resigns, the next in line on the Party list of the preceding election – in other words, the previously unsuccessful Party candidate who had won the most votes in that election - would accede automatically.

## Attendance and remuneration

Members of the House of Lords would be obliged to observe certain rules of attendance and would therefore be paid salaries and expenses. These would be fixed and revised from time to time by a Committee of the House of Commons, presided over by the Clerk of the Parliaments, to ensure neutrality and adequate consultation between the two Houses.

## Expected results from such a system

It would not be especially useful to try to predict or simulate the results of the elections to the House of Lords under a system such as that proposed above. It is clear, however, that the composition of the reformed House of Lords will seldom, if ever, correspond exactly to that of the House of Commons.

There are two reasons for this. First, the relative weightings proposed for Regional Lords and Party Lords would differ from those for Constituency and Party MPs in the Commons. Second, the timing of elections to the two Houses is unlikely to coincide.

A further consideration is that the age and maturity of the new Lords (if the suggested minimum age-bar is implemented) would make them less dependent on their Parties and less inclined to bow to Party lines. The possible presence of Independent Lords, likewise on the basis discussed earlier, would similarly help to give the reformed House of Lords a different and distinctive voice.

The greater independence which the House of Lords would have as a result of all these factors should enhance the value of their revising function. The debates in the Lords would continue to command respect and attention by the House of Commons and the public at large.

## Transitional arrangements

Finally, it would be important to implement the transition from the present House of Lords to a wholly elected chamber in such a way as to relieve a possible constitutional limbo and smooth the path of reform.

One way of easing the process would be to start by electing just half the members of the reformed House through the new, TR-based constituency system. 100 Regional Lords and 50 Party Lords could be elected in this way for the first six-year term.

The remaining half of the initial members could be internally elected by the members of the present House. Following the precedent set by Tony Blair and Lord Cranborne when reducing the number of Hereditary Peers, members of the present House could elect from among themselves 150 Lords (both hereditary and life-peers) who would stay behind. These Members too could continue to serve for six years to ensure continuity and help initiate their new, elected counterparts.

Six years later, the first full national election of 300 Lords (200 Regional Lords and 100 Party Lords) would take place, producing a wholly elected chamber.

Alternatively, if it were decided that elections for half the members of the reformed House should take place every three years, the initial cohort of 150 internally elected peers could serve for three years and a national election for their successors (whose terms would last six years) could take place at that point.

The Clerk of the Parliaments could be tasked, with help from some members of both Houses, to decide which 100 Regional Constituencies chosen from north to south would be the first half to hold elections

A remaining question is what would best be done with the remaining Life Peers and Hereditary Peers who are not elected in this way but would like to continue as Members of the House.

There is a simple, creative answer. The political Parties, which choose, delegate, or appoint their candidates for election in the regional constituencies, could give priority to deserving sitting Peers within their Parties. These Peers would then have a chance of remaining in the reformed Chamber as Regional Lords or as Party Lords within the Party lists. Even if they failed to capture regional seats, their efforts would be rewarded if they score highly in the regions and thus propel themselves to the top of their Party lists within the TR system. Their chances of acceding to the posts of Party Lords would depend as much on their own reputations and canvassing efforts as on the support of their Parties.

Last, but not least, what about the titles of Lord and Baroness? It would be for Parliament to resolve whether members of the new House should be designated in this way. If the decision is that they should, then it would seem fitting that they should be allowed to retain their titles for life after their terms of office expire.

# EPILOGUE
## *by Andrew Edwards*

We hope that the reader who has persevered thus far will agree on the importance of the subjects which this book discusses.

There are of course all manner of other troublesome issues which our country faces, such as the quest for independence in Scotland, the constitutional messes created by the Scottish Parliament, the Welsh Assembly and devolution generally, the divisive Brexit and EU issues and the inappropriate uses and specifications of Referendums, not to mention the mindless pursuit at certain times of politically correct multiculturalism at the expense of cohesion.

In our opinion, successive Governments have mishandled all these issues in recent years, making our once-successful society distinctly more vulnerable than before.

So Parliamentary democracy and the central electoral systems which are our principal focus in this book are certainly not the only challenges the country faces, and we would not wish for a moment to suggest that reforms like those we have outlined would solve all the problems of social cohesion which the country now faces or remove all the threats to our society.

We do believe, however, that reforms on these lines have a vital contribution to make in these all-important areas. Without such reforms, we fear that the tensions in our society, and the shift of focus from Parliament to street, from Westminster to Trafalgar Square, will escalate.

There are two final points which we would make, or re-iterate, about our suggested reforms, before concluding.

First, they all form part of a *single vision, based on preserving what is good (or very good) in the Westminster system while making some small but vital additions at the margin.*

In the Commons, the present FPTP electoral system for Constituency MPs would be maintained intact, with all its strengths, as would the constituencies themselves and the CMPs' traditional role of representing all their constituents. But the addition of a small but significant minority of Party MP seats, allocated to Parties in proportion to their shares of wasted votes and then to the individual candidates from the Party lists who have won the most votes, could provide representation for all voters and achieve a reasonable degree of proportionality overall.

In the Lords, the firm intention would be substantially to maintain as many as possible of the traditional strengths of the Upper Chamber (not least the legislating, revising and delaying roles, the cross-bench tradition and the professional experience and expertise). But the Chamber would be smaller and wholly elected, after some sensitively calibrated transitional arrangements, with a system for election similar to that for the Commons but with larger constituencies consisting of three Commons constituencies.

The system for Parliamentary elections would remain simple, transparent and familiar (unlike the bewildering multiplicity and complexity of electoral systems now introduced in other contexts in the UK), with voters casting one vote in their constituencies in the traditional way. It would be evolutionary, not revolutionary. It would go with the grain of our history and tradition.

The new, TR-based additions to our present system would be flexible. Parliament would decide after discussion on the relative numbers of CMPs and PMPs and on the coverage of the wasted votes to be used as a basis for allocating quotas of PMP seats to Parties. PMPs as well as CMPs would be personally elected by constituency voters.

The Parties would be encouraged to elect their Leaders according to the same philosophy and principles of Total Representation by means of the simple, transparent and beautiful system explained in Chapter 2.

Second, and finally, we believe there to ʼ be an overwhelming case for implementing reforms along the lines our book suggests as soon as possible, in the spirit of "action this day".

The reforms of House of Commons Elections in particular should be implemented alongside the re-drawing of constituencies (and their reduction from 650 to 600) which the Boundary Commissions have been mandated to complete in 2018.

As discussed in the Introduction, the proposed reforms could hardly be simpler in terms of legislation or practical execution. Our constitutional arrangements are such that, if the will is there, Parliament could legislate for them in a normal Act of Parliament.

In practical terms, they could readily be introduced alongside the new constituency boundaries. General Elections would proceed in exactly the same way as now. Voters would vote for CMPs in exactly the same way as they have voted for MPs in the past. The only difference would be that a number of PMP seats chosen by Parliament and included in the legislation would be allocated to Parties in proportion to "wasted" votes cast in the Election, and then to individual candidates, in accordance with the simple procedure discussed in Chapter 2.

As also discussed in the Introduction, however, securing agreement even to gentle, evolutionary reforms such as these, sensitively developed as they may be and extremely simple to introduce, is likely to be a challenge.

Parliament, Government and Parties will all wish, quite understandably, to receive, examine and discuss in depth any proposals for reform in this area before agreeing to them.

That being so, we believe that the best way ahead will be for Parliament to establish a high-powered Independent Commission straight away so as to set the ball rolling.

Some 20 years after the missed opportunity of the Jenkins Commission, therefore, we have recommended the immediate establishment of such a Commission, suitably constituted and supported, and including people of the highest integrity, ability and experience, with a remit:

*to review the issues of representation and other problems which presently beset our democratic institutions, practices and electoral systems, and to identify sensible options for reform – evolutionary and non-disruptive options such as those discussed in this book not least – with due assessment of their merits and demerits.*

The Commission should be firmly mandated, we suggest, to report within one year. All being well, its Report would provide an effective basis for national decisions thereafter on what should be done, with implementation alongside the newly re-drawn constituencies ahead of the probable date of the next General Election.

We would hope that the Commission's remit would cover all the issues discussed in this book, including House of Lords reform, systems for electing Party leaders and the role and conduct of Referendums, as well as elections to the House of Commons.

The Commission would do well, in our view, to give special attention to *coherent* packages of reform such as those discussed in previous Chapters.

Part of the reason why progress in these areas has been so limited in recent years is that there has been no BIG IDEA to help point the way forward.

In our view, such an idea is badly needed. Without it, stimulus, excitement and impetus will all be in short supply, and progress will continue to be difficult.

We venture to hope that the simple, original suggestions put forward in this book for preserving all that is good in our present systems but adding some limited, gentle yet significant reforms alongside under the banner of Total Representation, no votes being wasted, might just possibly provide the kind of big idea, or family of ideas, that is needed.

# ABOUT THE AUTHORS

**Andrew Edwards** worked at the Treasury for over 30 years from 1963 to 1995. As Under Secretary and then Deputy Secretary (Director General) on the public expenditure side and Chairman of the Government Finance Directors Committee, he was heavily involved in public expenditure planning and management, public sector and local government reforms and EU matters.

After leaving the Treasury, he served as Professional Adviser to many overseas Governments, especially the Governments of former communist countries, as they sought to develop democratic systems and modern industrial economies.

Within the UK, he has continued to work on issues of national importance, leading major Reviews of the British Museum, Financial Regulation in the Crown Dependencies and the Land Registry, chairing the inter-departmental Acacia Programme, acting as professional adviser to the Greenbury Committee on Directors' Pay, and more recently leading about 80 Gateway Reviews of major Government policies and programmes.

Previous publications include *Nuclear Weapons, the Balance of Terror, the Quest for Peace* (Macmillan, 1985).

**Aharon Nathan** entered the civil service in Israel in 1954 and joined the team of advisers to Prime Ministers Ben Gurion and Moshe Sharett.

In 1955 he was appointed by Ben Gurion as Secretary to Yohanan Rattner Commission on the future administration of Arab areas in Israel. In 1956 he was appointed Secretary to Judge Azulai's fact-finding Commission on the Kafr Qasim massacre which drew the distinction between lawful and unlawful orders for future engagement rules of the army. Following the Suez War he set up and headed the first civil administration in Gaza.

In the early 1960s he was in charge of integrating the Arab workers as full members of the Histadrut Trade Union and coordinated Mapai Party general elections in the Arab sector. Prompted by Ben Gurion's desire to adopt the Westminster electoral System, he then left for Oxford and there formulated Total Representation (TR) as a more suitable system to answer the divisions that were inherent in Israel's diverse society. After leaving Oxford he remained in the UK pursuing a career in business which led to him travelling extensively throughout the Far East and Eastern Europe.

In 2005 he was appointed by the President of Israel to the Commission to examine the government and governance of the country. The Commission adopted the principles of TR in its final Report. Following that together with Prof Gideon Doron the President of the Political Association in Israel, he prepared three draft laws which were tabled in three successive Knessets.

34174761R00077

Printed in Great Britain
by Amazon